Children's Conceptions of Health, Illness, and Bodily Functions

Roger Bibace, Mary E. Walsh, *Editors*

NEW DIRECTIONS FOR CHILD DEVELOPMENT
WILLIAM DAMON, *Editor-in-Chief*

Number 14, December 1981

Paperback sourcebooks in
The Jossey-Bass Social and Behavioral Sciences Series

Jossey-Bass Inc., Publishers
San Francisco • Washington • London

Children's Conceptions of Health, Illness, and Bodily Functions
Number 14, 1981, December 1981
Roger Bibace, Mary E. Walsh, *Editors*

New Directions for Child Development Series
William Damon, *Editor-in-Chief*

New Directions for Child Development (publication number
USPS 494-090) is published quarterly by Jossey-Bass Inc., Publishers.
Second-class postage rates are paid at San Francisco, California,
and at additional mailing offices.

Correspondence:
Subscriptions, single-issue orders, change of address notices,
undelivered copies, and other correspondence should be sent to
New Directions Subscriptions, Jossey-Bass Inc., Publishers,
433 California Street, San Francisco, California 94104.

Editorial correspondence should be sent to the Editor-in-Chief,
William Damon, Department of Psychology, Clark University,
Worcester, Massachusetts 01610.

Library of Congress Catalogue Card Number LC 81-48241
International Standard Serial Number ISSN 0195-2269
International Standard Book Number ISBN 87589-804-1

Cover art by Willi Baum
Manufactured in the United States of America

Ordering Information

The paperback sourcebooks listed below are published quarterly and can be ordered either by subscription or single-copy.

Subscriptions cost $30.00 per year for institutions, agencies, and libraries. Individuals can subscribe at the special rate of $18.00 per year *if payment is by personal check.* (Note that the full rate of $30.00 applies if payment is by institutional check, even if the subscription is designated for an individual.) Standing orders are accepted.

Single copies are available at $6.95 when payment accompanies order, and *all single-copy orders under $25.00 must include payment.* (California, Washington, D.C., New Jersey, and New York residents please include appropriate sales tax.) For billed orders, cost per copy is $6.95 plus postage and handling. (Prices subject to change without notice.)

To ensure correct and prompt delivery, all orders must give either the *name of an individual* or an *official purchase order number.* Please submit your order as follows:

Subscriptions: specify series and subscription year.
Single Copies: specify sourcebook code and issue number (such as, CD8).

Mail orders for United States and Possessions, Latin America, Canada, Japan, Australia, and New Zealand to:
Jossey-Bass Inc., Publishers
433 California Street
San Francisco, California 94104

Mail orders for all other parts of the world to:
Jossey-Bass Limited
28 Banner Street
London EC1Y 8QE

New Directions for Child Development Series
William Damon, *Editor-in-Chief*

Contents

Editors' Notes

During the past twenty-five years or so, socialization theories have become increasingly influenced by developmental approaches such as those of Piaget and Werner. The significance of this influence lies in a shift in our perception of children. From a view of children as little adults, gradually building the data base of information required to be a socialized member of society, we have moved to an appreciation that what children know about life is qualitatively different from what adults know. This implies that it is not simply the case that children know *less* about the world than adults or that their views can be judged as right or wrong according to an adult measurement scale; the cognitive apparatus with which they perceive and conceptualize the world is different, and it is the task of developmental psychologists to understand it.

This distinction between the child as a passive recipient of environmental information and the child as an agent, actively constructing his or her own views, becomes especially relevant in the study of the health-related issues represented by the chapters in this volume. Birth, death, medical procedures, health, illness, and body interior are issues about which children tend to vocalize spontaneously because they have to do with the child's own body and are of great personal concern to him or her. This may be in contrast to other social domains previously studied by developmental psychologists, in which children's conceptions often must be inferred from their behavior. Friendship, for example, is certainly important to the child, but it is rarely associated with the personal urgency attached to health-related issues and thus less likely to prompt spontaneous verbalization. Because children's conceptions of health-related issues are articulated more often, the logic underlying them can be readily evaluated by adults, and the sharp contrast between the child's and the adult's conceptions becomes obvious. A common statement such as, "To get a baby, you go to the store and buy a duck," is then typically judged by parents, teachers, and health care professionals as quaint, weird, cute, random, or simply wrong.

This is the starting point for these chapters. In each case, the major thrust of the study is that the comments children make regarding health-related issues that appear on the surface to be cute, silly, or haphazard, actually are part of an orderly developmental sequence of knowledge. This means first,

We gratefully acknowledge the assistance of Mira Zamansky Schorin and Karen Cammuso in the preparation of the manuscript.

that a particular type of response will predominate within a certain general age group and, more importantly, that the formal aspects of the responses correspond to the mental structures that determine how the world in general is conceived. In such responses, the cardinal dimension for assessing development is the degree of differentiation between self and other. This central theme cuts across all the content areas addressed in this volume, as well as every approach to a developmental analysis of formal aspects of reasoning. As both of us, as well as Bernstein and Cowan, point out in our chapter, this approach stands in contrast to the psychoanalytic approach, which has sought to account for children's conceptions of health in terms of fear of punishment and to account for children's conceptions of birth and sexuality in terms of the dynamics of the Oedipal conflict and children's immature sexual equipment. We stress that the psychoanalytic view is too limited a basis for explanation of the variety of children's responses. Furthermore, at a formal level, children's conceptions of health-related issues need not be interpreted any differently from their conceptions of other domains of life.

Investigation into children's conceptions of health-related issues poses some of the same problems, theoretical, methodological, and clinical, that confront studies of children's understanding within other domains, such as the social and the moral. However, this area of research does have exclusive rights to certain theoretical, methodological, and clinical problems concerning childhood and health. Both of us and the other authors of these chapters address many of these issues and suggest a number of different ways of approaching them. While all of us concur on the general task of articulating the developmental sequence of children's thinking about one or another of these health-related phenomena, we do not always agree about every theoretical, methodological, and clinical issue of concern.

One of the most pervasive theoretical issues in cognitive-developmental research, one that is raised by all of us, is the nature of the relationship between cognition and affect. This issue demands special attention in the area of health because of its great potential for evoking an emotional response in young subjects. The clinical interview is the most popular, but not the exclusive, technique for eliciting data among these chapters (note Steward and Steward's presentation of medical instruments to subjects and Crider's reliance on subjects' drawings), and theoretical interview has been often used to insulate the subject's response from the affective influences of "real life." The interview, however, is ineffective in health-related issues from which an affective component may be inextricable, such as in a discussion of sexuality (see Bernstein and Cowan) or a discussion of death by a child who is himself seriously ill (see Koocher). While the effect of affect on children's thinking is generally assumed to be detrimental, Steward and Steward suggest that affect may influence children differentially, depending on cognitive level. In addition, Koocher maintains that a developmental progression may still be evaluated independently of affective influences. At the same time, however, he warns researchers to be sensitive to the negative feelings that questions about death may elicit in young subjects.

Another central issue confronting we authors is whether the level of cognitive maturity evidenced in a child's response in one domain correlates with some other measure of his or her cognitive ability in another domain. This raises the questions of whether there can be an independent measure of the level of cognitive development and, if so, what the appropriate indicator should be. Studies of children's conceptions of physical domains do not address these questions because it is assumed that the content of these domains is fundamental to all other areas of thought. Investigators of the development of conceptions of health-related issues maintain that such content areas are less fundamental and, consequently, some find it necessary to use an independent measure of developmental status. In the attempt to find an unbiased developmental indicator, these researchers would seem to be struggling with the perennial issue of how to extract form from content. The authors of this volume address this problem in a number of ways. Koocher, for example, correlates children's conceptions of death with their performance on standard Piagetian tasks of cognitive development such as conservation, so that the preoperational child should show the least advanced understanding of death, and formal-operational children should show the most advanced understanding. Others begin by assessing the child's developmental status with respect to certain forms of reasoning (for example, identity) that are assumed to be fundamental to the health-related concept. These assessments are made in what the researchers consider to be a relatively neutral content domain. Bernstein and Cowan, for example, measure children's developing understanding of causality and identity with respect to both physical and social objects, since these concepts are considered central to the issues of birth and sexuality. Both of us, however, maintain that there cannot be an indicator variable that is independent of a content of some kind. We argue against the assumption that assessment of cognitive functioning on a task whose content is distantly related to the domain of experimental interest (such as a child's understanding of rain as an indicator of his or her understanding of illness) qualifies as a pure indicator that is in effect content-free. Since form and content can never be disentangled, we, with a normal population of children, prefer to use age as a rough indicator of cognitive level on the health-related issue, acknowledging that predictions based on age are not always accurate.

However, developmental psychologists are well aware that age is not a perfect index of cognitive functioning, even among groups of normal children.

This is because there is a great deal of variation among children of the same age. The variability in children's level of understanding requires the consideration of other variables. Some variables already addressed by researchers include mode of presenting the task, the task characteristics, such subject variables as the affective status of the subject, or an interaction between the two — for example, the subject's familiarity with the type of stimulus material being used (see, for example, Kagan and Kogan, 1970). Thus, cognitive development cannot be fully understood without an appreciation of the role of individual differences — that is, without taking into account what is referred to as between-subject variation.

A related but separate issue concerns variability in levels of reasoning manifested by a single subject within a single content area (within-subject variability). It was Piaget who labeled this issue as décalage (Flavell, 1963). This variability gives rise to a methodological problem when one attempts to assign children to a single stage, even though they evidence reasoning reflecting more than one developmental level. In our chapter, we discuss two scoring options available when a single score or stage is sought: taking as the child's score the average of scores at different levels or taking the highest level of reasoning used consistently by the child. Both of these methods are used throughout these chapters.

Another methodological problem emerges when one attempts to articulate the developmental categories for a particular content area. Crider argues for utilizing the formal qualities of responses as a criterion for forming categories or stages. Crider emphasizes the danger of using the model response within an age group as the stage criterion. She also makes a case for doing away with the term *stage* in favor of *level of conceptualization,* which does not carry the theoretical surplus meaning attached to stages. The existence of stages, in the strictest sense of the term, can only be verified empirically through a scalogram on cross-sectional data. While the chapter authors recognize this problem, none of them makes use of either of these options. Koocher, for example, is quick to point out the need for longitudinal data in order to establish a developmental sequence of children's conceptions of death with confidence.

Other scoring difficulties, as well as other methodological and theoretical problems, both stated and unstated, become apparent within these chapters. It is easy to see how quickly the complexity of research increases when the topic of investigation moves away from the domain of physical reality to more conspicuous or personally relevant aspects of our daily lives. It is also important to note here that a variety of theoretical and methodological approaches to studying children's conceptions of health-related issues may be necessary due to differences in the nature of the areas being studied. All health-related domains may not share identical properties, so that a particular approach is not necessarily desirable in every case. Death, for example, may be a concept that is differently understood by children at different ages, but its manifestation, the event itself, does not change with age. In the case of sexuality, however, it is not only that the understanding of an identical phenomenon changes with age, but that, as Bernstein and Cowan suggest, sexuality may in fact be something of a different phenomenon for young and old in terms of the locus and nature of pleasure. In studying death, then, it is appropriate to ask children of different ages about death with fair confidence that the same "thing" is being studied across time and to connect responses along developmental lines to adults' conceptions. This is in fact the approach and interpretation found in Koocher's study of children's conceptions of death. Regarding sexuality, however, it may be worthwhile not only to look for the precursors of the child's understanding of adult sexuality — that is, intercourse — but to characterize how sexuality is experienced by the child at different ages. This suggestion refers more to sexuality itself than to the concept of reproduction upon which Bernstein and Cowan focus. Nevertheless, this issue remains relevant for all researchers studying children's developing conceptions of health-related issues. It is necessary to consider whether or not the concept under investigation manifests itself differently at varying points in development.

The present chapters are all reflective of the burgeoning interest of developmental psychologists in social cognition. Moreover, each study addresses a content area of central concern to helping professionals who work with children. It is not coincidental that all the authors of these chapters are either practicing clinicians or developmental psychologists who work with professionals in diverse clinical contexts. While recognizing the theoretical significance of their investigations, the authors are also keenly aware of the practical relevance of new insights into how children think in terms of their implications for health education curricula and improved communication and understanding between health-care practitioners and patients. Distinctively, the present studies have yielded results that are theoretically sound and clinically useful. They are valid theoretically insofar as the data, children's responses about health-related issues, were found to change as a function of age and to reflect the structural properties in the child's cognitive processes.

In clinical settings, such data can be used directly by health-care professionals who previously were limited to applying, in an indirect manner, the general principles of developmental psychology. That is, practitioners have been restricted by the commonly held misconception that in order to apply theoretical findings in clinical settings, one need only use them in these settings. For example, physicians have believed that an awareness of the preoperational, concrete-, and formal-operational stages of children's cognitive development should inform their encounters with young patients who express fears or who ask questions about medical procedures. But the problem is that theoretical knowledge of general cognitive processes does not directly or easily transfer to clinical settings. A child's response about a particular issue cannot be automatically interpreted in terms of a general developmental framework. Even experienced developmental psychologists who are very well versed in the formal characteristics of general developmental stages are unable to predict the content of a response at a given level within a specific domain. How, then, could practicing physicians, far less familiar with general developmental principles, be expected to make effective use of them in their own practices? Prior to the works in the present volume, the main body of developmental studies has offered only such general theoretical principles.

The studies in this sourcebook have also tried to avoid the other extreme, in which subjects' responses are simply presented as they occurred—for example, catalogued in some tabular form, without any attempt made to tie them to a formal theoretical system. This approach appears equally useless for clinicians, who themselves have plentiful personal access to examples of the kinds of things children say. The real issue is how to help the clinician help his or her clients by understanding more about the responses they make.

Thus, a worthwhile aspect of these studies is that they have managed to integrate the theoretical and clinical spheres by making concrete basic cognitive processes in health-related domains. The sequence of responses described in each study relfects not only the formal characteristics of cognitive stages but also the *content* of the health-related issues under investigation, a classification system we denote as "task relevant categories." The studies demonstrate how it is possible for developmental psychology to be used in clinical settings in a direct and meaningful way.

Because these categories are to be used in clinical contexts, a question remains as to how broadly or narrowly the task in task-relevant categories should be defined. The answer to this question depends on who, within the clinical domain, is to be served by the investigation into children's understanding: generalists (such as clinical development specialists or family physicians who are not limited by the age of the patient or the type of illness) versus specialists (such as clinical neuropsychologists, pediatric neurologists, or cardiologists). For example, studies that focus on conceptions of illness, none of which are defined any more broadly than heart disease, are unlikely to yield results of great use to the cardiologist in dealing with his or her patients. The clinical developmental psychologist, however, may argue that such studies are already too constricted to provide results of general significance.

These studies, taken together, testify to the potency of an analysis of children's reasoning according to a developmental framework. This approach is seen to transcend the domains of birth, death, health and illness, medical procedures, and body interior by providing a single framework by which to interpret children's conceptions across all these domains. All the studies offer rich examples of children's thoughts about these health-related issues and clearly indicate how these thoughts can be ordered along a developmental continuum of cognitive maturity. Clinically, the studies recognize that, to use developmental theory, practitioners must be able to match theoretical findings with their own clinical experience. Moreover, these authors are sensitive to the practitioner's primary concern of gaining an appreciation of the way in which a particular child thinks about a certain content area, in contrast to the researcher's goal of assigning the child to a particular stage. The authors assume that the empathy of practitioners will be facilitated if they better understand how patients, young and old, are viewing their situation. Practitioners themselves may come to understand the kinds of changes their own thoughts undergo when they find themselves in unfamiliar or stressful situations. For example, what hospitalized developmental psychologist has not temporarily entertained some body or health-related notions that could be characterized as immature?

This emphasis on what is occurring for the practitioners in their attempts to deal with patients indicates that the patient is not the sole focus on interest in these studies. Just as developmentalists traditionally view the child's development as a function of interactions between child and environment, so too the chapters in this volume are focused on the interaction between practitioner and client. Each is an active participant and potential beneficiary of the interaction.

Roger Bibace
Mary E. Walsh
Editors

References

Flavell, J. H. *The Developmental Psychology of Jean Piaget.* Princeton, N.J.: D. Van Nostrand, 1963.
Kagan, J., and Kogan, N. "Individuality and Cognitive Performance." In P. Mussen (Ed.), *Carmichael's Manual of Child Psychology.* Wiley, 1970.

Roger Bibace is professor of psychology at Clark University and adjunct professor in the Department of Family and Community Medicine, University of Massachusetts Medical Center, Worcester.

Mary E. Walsh is associate professor of psychology at Regis College and an adjunct associate professor in the Department of Family and Community Medicine, University of Massachusetts Medical Center, Worcester.

"If daddy put his egg in you, I must be a chicken," three-year-old Seth told his mother. "To get a baby, you go to the store and buy a duck," explained four-year-old Susan. Children's ideas about sex and birth are not for the birds; however, they follow a Piagetian developmental sequence.

Children's Conceptions of Birth and Sexuality

Anne C. Bernstein
Philip A. Cowan

Storks fly through the air dangling babies from diaper slings. Cabbage patches are filled with infants hidden among the leaves. Doctors pull forth babies from black bags. Are these images of birth based on childhood imagination or misinformation? Sex educators have often assumed that childhood myths are created when embarrassed parents use euphemisms to avoid a direct discussion of sex. But if Piaget's cognitive-developmental approach is relevant to understanding how babies come into being, then there should be a regular developmental sequence of ideas about babies—a sequence in which children often make up their own answers or assimilate what they have been told to their general cognitive level. In other words, ideas about babies should be embedded in a matrix of other ideas that children construct to make sense of their physical and social world.

We would like to thank Ellen Nannis for her literature search, Claire Brindis for supplying much of the background material on adolescent sexuality, and Carolyn Cowan for her comments on an earlier draft of the manuscript.

R. Bibace and M. Walsh (Eds.). *New Directions for Child Development: Childrens' Conceptions of Health, Illness, and Bodily Functions*, no. 14. San Francisco: Jossey-Bass, December 1981

That children do in fact make their own sense of the physical and social world is just what we found (Bernstein, 1978; Bernstein and Cowan, 1975) when one of us interviewed sixty male and female children between the ages of three and twelve. When we began to collect data for our study in 1972, we noted that developmental and personality theorists, sex educators, and the general public were all espousing very definite, different, and often contradictory views about the nature of childhood sexuality, what children already knew, and what they should be taught (Breasted, 1971). Adults on all sides of debates in both academic and applied arenas were arguing forcefully for their own interpretations without gathering information from children and adolescents themselves. Our study was designed as a beginning attempt to obtain this information and to examine the usefulness of Piaget's cognitive-developmental theory in understanding the results. In this chapter, we present a summary of our previous findings concerning children's ideas about conception and birth, supplemented by new observations about children's concepts of sexuality. These findings provide a background for a discussion of some central issues in theory, research, and application.

A Piagetian investigation of children's ideas about birth and sexuality is part of the growing attempt to extend Piagetian theory from its concern with the child's understanding of the physical world to the domain of social cognition. Noting the scarcity of subsequent research on the specific topic of childbirth and examining the complexity of methodological issues in this area, we will suggest that this research is still sensitive. Awkwardness and embarrassment are often displayed by sex educators in schools, by parents, and by researchers; these feelings are also evident in children who were interviewed for our study. Nevertheless, we believe that the research must be continued and extended. More than in most areas of development, the child's understanding of birth and sexuality involves cognition, emotion, and social-interpersonal behavior. These aspects, which have generally been studied separately, can be brought together to enrich our understanding of the whole child. Further, the design of programs of sex education in schools and planned parenthood clinics and the effectiveness of parental instruction at home can be enhanced by more explicit attempts to match what is taught to the level of the learner. These are issues that will be discussed more fully after a presentation of the background and data from our own study.

Background

Because psychologists have speculated about children's ideas about sex and birth without seeking the child's own views, many of the theories about the child's view of procreation have involved projections of adult thinking. Early psychoanalytic writings, probably the most bountiful sources of ideas about childhood sexuality, rely only secondarily on direct observation and questioning of children. Freud (1963) admitted that his sources in reconstructing the sexual theories of children were primarily: (1) the screened memories of childhood that adult neurotics recovered during psychoanalysis and (2) his own unconscious memories, reconstructed into consciousness in the course of treating his patients.

Some descriptions of the child's Oedipal conflicts read as if four-year-olds have very accurate ideas about parents' sexual practices and the creation of babies, but Freud also states that a child's understanding of reproduction is limited by his or her physiological immaturity. Anna Freud (1965) presents a similar argument. The immaturity of the infantile sexual apparatus leaves the child "no choice" but to translate adult genital happenings into pregenital events, the "age-appropriate terms of orality and anality, violence and mutilations" (p. 59).

Piaget (1960a), writing twenty years later than Freud, focused not on physiological immaturity but on the cognitive-structural apparatus as the system through which children transform incoming information. He agreed with Freud about the importance of childhood concepts of conception and speculated that "in all probability it is the curiosity concerning birth which is the starting point of questions of origin" (p. 367) and a primary impetus to the development of ideas about causality. But Piaget believed that there were "grave moral and pedagogical reasons" (p. 360) for not pursuing a direct investigation of children's thinking about the origins of natural phenomena (that is, night, wind, clouds, and so forth). He assumed that their ideas about the cause of babies should follow the same sequence of developmental stages as their general concepts of physical causality.

Between 1929 and 1975, outside the psychoanalytic tradition of case studies, three systematic empirical studies explored children's ideas of where babies came from. Conn (1947) used doll-play interviews with 100 four-year-old children; he reported the content of their answers and used none of the probes necessary to code the responses according to cognitive-structural criteria for stages or levels. His conclusions—that preschoolers do not know that the baby is in the mother and sex information is beyond the grasp of the intelligent seven- or eight-year-old—seem outmoded in view of what young children talk about today.

More recently, Kreitler and Kreitler (1966) and Moore and Kendall (1971) set out to test Piaget's hypothesis about the connection between cognitive stage and ideas about babies. The age range of the children tested was narrow (4 to 5:6; 3 to 5:6), interview probes were not extensive, and no tasks were used to provide markers of cognitive level independent of age. When they found no evidence of the artificialist thinking typical of preoperational children, both sets of authors prematurely dismissed Piaget's hypothesis about the connection between causal thinking and sexual enlightenment.

In our study (Bernstein and Cowan, 1975), we felt that it was important to investigate a much wider age range. Specifically, we wanted to know whether children's concepts of procreation followed a Piagetian stage sequence and whether their ideas about babies were closely related to the development of concepts in other content areas. It seemed to us that the cognitive concepts most relevant to the origin of babies are those concerning causality and identity. It is only when the child begins to perceive that events and phenomena have causes that he or she can attempt to investigate what they are; it is only when chldren recognize that they themselves and other people as well are continuous beings, conserving identity despite the transformations in appearance, that they can think about their own origins or those of their siblings.

Method

In order to explore the general hypothesis that children's concepts of reproduction are embedded in a cognitive-developmental matrix, we included tasks to assess and compare children's developing understanding of causality and identity with respect to both physical and social objects. The development of physical identity was inferred from children's performance in the traditional conservation interview involving transformations of clay. (At that time we were not clear about Piaget's distinction between identity and conservation [1968]). A measure developed by Lemke (1973), as yet unpublished, was used to assess the child's sense that an individual's social identity continues through time despite changes in physical appearance. Concepts of physical causality were assessed by use of Laurendeau and Pinard's (1962) standardized version of Piaget's interviews (1960a) about the origin of night. An analogous interview was constructed to discover children's thinking about the origin of babies (social causality). In retrospect it seems to us that the task represents a combination of social and physical causality concepts.

Twenty boys and girls at each of three age levels (three/four, seven/eight, and eleven/twelve) were interviewed and tested. These ages were selected to elicit performance levels ranging from preoperational through concrete-operational to the beginnings of formal-operational thought.

Given the hesitance of many parents to have their children questioned about sexual matters, random sampling was not attempted. The final sample, referred by our acquaintances and community nursery schools, consisted primarily of middle and upper-middle class Caucasian children. All had at least one younger sibling and thus would have had to cope with the entrance of a younger child into their families. Because the study focused on establishing invariant sequences of performance and within-individual developmental cohesion, the lack of random sampling was not considered a serious drawback at this stage of our knowledge.

Each child was approached as a consultant and asked to aid the interviewer in her work, which, she explained, was learning how children think. After securing the child's agreement and after a warm-up period, the interviewer began with a question: "How do people get babies?" The child's response was then questioned until he or she had followed through on the implications of his or her initial explanation. Each answer was probed until the child's answer became as explicit and as detailed as he or she was able to make it. It was not assumed that the children's use of any given word necessarily meant that they comprehended the common usage definition.

Each interview included the following questions: How do people get babies? What does the word *born* mean? What does it mean to say someone was born? How do mothers get to be mothers? How did your mother get to be *your* mother? How do fathers get to be fathers? How did your father get to be *your* father? When did he start being your father? How was it that (name of younger sibling) came to live in your family and be your sister/brother?

In addition, younger children were asked, "What if some people, who lived in a cave in the desert where there weren't any other people, wanted to have a baby? Because they had never known any other people, they didn't know how people get babies. What if they asked you for help? If they asked you what they should do if they wanted a baby, what would you tell them?"

Older children were asked, "What did you think about how people get babies before you understood it as well as you do now? What did you think when you were little?"

Origins of Babies: A Seven-Level Scale

Pilot protocols (n = 25) were used to create a scale with scores ranging from 0–6. Following the structural outline of Laurendeau and Pinard's physical causality scale (1962), it dealt specifically with the application of similar levels of cognitive development to the problem of the origin of babies.

Level 0: Lack of Comprehension of Questions. (This was true of only five of the three- to four-year-olds and none of the remaining children.)

Level 1: The Geographers. These preoperational children (60 percent of the three- and four-year-olds in our sample; 30 percent of the seven- and eight-year olds) interpret the question How do people get babies? as spatial, not causal; it becomes, *Where* do people get babies? Like Dennis the Menace, who watches movies of his parents' wedding and then complains, "I guess I was home with the sitter while you were having all the fun," these children cannot conceive of a time when they did not exist. The only question that is real (to them) is where the baby was before it came to live with their parents. The location may vary: "You go to the baby store and buy one" (3:8), "You get them from hospitals" (3:6), "From God's place" (4:1), "From tummies" (3:2).

Further probes reveal no first cause: "It just grows inside mommy's tummy. It's there all the time. Mommy doesn't have to do anything. She just waits until she feels it."

Level 2: The Manufacturers. Although still preoperational by other measures and by age (30 percent of the 3:4 age group), these children answer the how question as such. Recognizing that babies have not always existed, they attribute babies to some cause, primarily a person or people who function as manufacturers. Artificialism, in which the origin of natural phenomena is described as if they have been manufactured, here entails only the use of natural materials. Jane (3:7), for example, explained, "You just make the baby first. You put some eyes on it. You put the head on, and hair, some hair all curls. You make it with head stuff. You find a store that makes it. . . . Well, they get it, and they put it in the tummy and then it goes quickly out."

Still egocentric, these children can interpret the world only in terms of events or processes they have themselves experienced. Therefore, they often fall into the digestive fallacy and believe that babies are conceived by swallowing and born by elimination.

The few children who connect a father with procreation assimilate what they have been told to a mechanical process. One four-year-old girl said, "He puts his hand in his tummy and gets it (the seed) and puts it on the bottom of the mommy, and the mommy gets the egg out of her tummy and puts the egg on top of the seed. And then they close their tummies and the baby is born." For her the seed and the egg can only come together by manual means. She expressed some doubts about her hypothesis, saying, "Cause the daddy can't really open up all his tummies," but her experience provided her with no real alternatives. In our interviews, we found no evidence that these young children make a connection between the sexual activity of their parents and the appearance of a baby. We shall discuss this point later on.

This example and others we will cite begin to illustrate a general conclusion: knowledge about babies and, we will argue later, knowledge about sex are not simply a matter of information and misinformation. It is difficult to believe that children have somehow been told the answers they give; rather, it appears that children who wonder about or are asked about the origin of babies make up answers. Their answers represent assimilations both from the content of experience and from the structure of thought.

Level 3: In Transition. Children at this level (40 percent of the seven-to eight-year-old sample) explain procreation as a mixture of physiology and technology, but they confine their explanations to operations that are technically feasible: They exclude such clearly unrealistic elements as "putting his hand in his tummy to get the seed." Parents no longer have the variety of ingredients available in the marketplace to help them make babies. They are limited to the contents of their own bodies for materials, although they have to depend on the doctor to supply the critical ingredient. Artificialism is expressed in muted form in accounts of embryonic development that resemble the fabrication of an item on an assembly line, as the baby is described as growing first a head, then a leg, and then an arm.

Literalness of thought leads to other distortions. One example is the agricultural fallacy, or the concretization of the metaphor of what the father does — "planting a seed" — which becomes "like a flower, I think, except you don't need dirt," according to one five-year-old. Animistic distortions are also prevalent at this stage (that is, attribution to nonliving things and to parts of living things the will and physical motility of people and animals). Jeanne, aged seven, says: "The sperm goes into the mommy to each egg and puts it, makes the egg safe. So if something bump comes along, it won't crack the egg. The sperm comes from the daddy. It swims into the penis, and I think it makes a little hole and then it swims into the vagina. It has a little mouth, and it bites a hole."

Children giving Level 3 responses appeared to have isolated three major ingredients in the creation of babies: social relationship (some effective and/or marital bond between man and woman), the external mechanics of sexual intercourse, and sperm-egg physiology. Children in this category conceptualize these ingredients in a more sophisticated way than those in Level 2. However, they are still consistent with the general description of children in transition between preoperations and concrete operations, as they are unable to coordinate any of the variables in a coherent system: Variables in one domain are assimilated to variables in another.

One example of this assimilation can be seen in eight-year-old Frank's responses: (His mother reports that he was taught sperm-egg physiology and about intercourse as a function of procreation and a love relationship.) "I guess it's like mothers and fathers are related, and their loving each other forms a baby. It's just there's love, and I guess it just forms a baby. I guess the love forms the beans, and I guess the beans hatches the egg." It would seem that Frank has absorbed more about the love relationship than about the physiology. The love between the baby's parents is not just an important part of their relationship but part of the substance of the baby itself, the clay from which it is molded.

Even children who describe sexual intercourse may still find the process mysterious. Ursula, at eight, describes how the father gives "the stuff" for the baby: "Well, he puts his penis right in the place where the baby comes out, and somehow it comes out of there. It seems like magic sort of, 'cause it just comes out. Sometimes I think the father pushes, maybe." She was somewhat vague in describing why his contribution is necessary: "If he didn't then a baby wouldn't come. Because it would need the stuff that the father gives. It helps it grow. I think that stuff has the food part, maybe, and maybe it helps protects it. I think he gives the shell part, and the shell part, I think, is the skin."

This example illustrates the possibility that social stereotypes of gender roles are being extended to the act of sex and the process of fertilization. Fathers, stereotypically seen as active protectors, are here viewed by Ursula literally as the prime movers in sex and as providing the outer covering of the egg that is later transformed into skin. It is our impression that many examples follow the same form: Ideas about sexual behavior and fertilization are assimilated to (transformed by) stereotypic gender role concepts. This sequence contrasts with Freud's implied sequence, in which male and female roles in the possession of sexual equipment and in making love are seen as leading to a natural order of gender roles (males as active, females as passive).

Level 4: Reporters. This is the first of three levels in which explanations rely completely on physical causes of conception. All the artificialism and mechanical manufacturing theories of Levels 1 and 2 are rejected. Variables are coordinated in a biological system. But Level 4 is distinguished from Levels 5 and 6 by the fact that at this stage the child cannot provide an explanation of the necessity of uniting genetic materials. Only 5 percent of the three- to four-year-olds in our sample reached level 4, while 30 percent of the seven- to eight-year-olds and 100 percent of the eleven- to twelve-year-olds were in the last three levels.

Seven-year-old Karen says, "The man and the woman get together, and then they put a speck, then the man has his seed and the woman has an egg, and then I guess, that's all I know really." When asked why the seed and the egg have to come together, she replied: "Or else the baby, the egg won't really get hatched very well. The seed makes the egg grow. It's just like plants; if you plant a seed, a flower will grow. It's a special kind of seed that makes an egg hatch." Asked if either seed or egg could grow into a baby without the other, she did not know.

Called reporters because of their concern for accuracy, children at this level are reluctant to speculate on the rationale behind the facts they have adopted on the strength of the authority of parents, teachers, or books. Although aware that there are things they do not understand, they rigorously exclude theorizing without evidence. At no other level of reasoning were children so hesitant to guess when they did not feel certain. Asked to explain the necessity of fertilization, many children simply describe sexual intercourse and assert flatly, "That's just the way people have their babies," or "That's the way I learned it." At this level, which corresponds with concrete operational thinking in other spheres, children are not yet ready to generate their own hypotheses.

Level 5: Theoreticians. Children at Level 5 are now willing to speculate about why sperm and ovum must unite to form new life. Going beyond rote repetition of the facts they have been taught, they arrive at theories that echo the history of scientific thinking about embryology. In this history the term preformation is used to refer to growth without differentiation—that is, the preexistence in miniature of all living creatures in the germ cells of animals and the seeds of plants. Not quite able to come up with an explanation of how two things can become one qualitatively different entity, Level 5 children see the baby as preformed in one germ cell; sexual intercourse merely provides necessary conditions for development to occur. Either the baby is said to be really in the ovum, needing the sperm only to catalyze its growth or give it energy (the ovist position), or, alternatively, it is the sperm that turns into a baby, given the nourishment and hospitable environment of the ovum (the animalculist position). In either case, the child still does not conceive of a stage before the baby's existence; its original substance is invariable, and there is no perceived need for a final cause.

For the ovists in our sample, sexual intercourse and fertilization are necessary so that the latent embryo in the egg can be energized or given life by the catalytic sperm. Twelve-year-old William, for example, describes fertilization: "That's when the sperm enters the egg. I guess the egg just has sort of an undeveloped embryo and when the sperm enters it, it makes it come to life. It gives it energy and things like that." Denying that the sperm can grow with no egg, he went on to explain, "That doesn't have the baby; it's the egg that would have the baby in it."

The animalculist position is structurally similar, but this time the baby is preformed in the sperm. Eleven-year-old Kathy describes sexual intercourse as necessary in order to transfer the sperm from its point origin in the father to an environment more conducive to development. Asked how fathers get to be fathers, she replied: "Well, if they're the man that made love to your mother then they're your father because you really originally came out of him, and then went into your mother. First you were a sperm inside of him, there. So that you're really his daughter or son, 'cause otherwise the sperm will have nothing to nourish it or sort of keep it warm or able to move or something. It just dies if it doesn't have the egg." Thus, the egg is described as having the stereotyped feminine cultural role of providing warmth and nourishment for the developing fetus.

These explicit explanations of ovism and animalculism demonstrate two important points. First, these eleven- to twelve-year-olds have a preformist notion of conception. But, in contrast with the notions of three- and four-year-olds, this notion is embedded in a much more complex causal theory. Like other aspects of Piaget's theory, development seems to occur in a spiral rather than a straight line. Children circle back to the same issues but, each time, deal with them on a more differentiated and integrated structural level. Second, these explanations suggest that children may recapitulate part of the history of the science of embryology in trying to make sense of human reproduction. The next step after Level 5, historically and ontogenetically, is the realization that the genetic material for the embryo is furnished by both parents and that the system is interactive rather than additive. Contrary to what is popularly expressed, the child is not simply a composite of his mother's eyes, his grandfather's ears, and his father's temper. It is possible that formal operations may be necessary for Level 6 explanations of the origin of babies.

Level 6: Putting It All Together. In order for children to be rated at Level 6 (40 percent of the eleven- to twelve-year-olds, 5 percent of the seven-to eight-year-olds), they had to include in their physiological explanations of reproduction the ideas that the embryo begins its biological existence at the moment of conception and that it is a product of genetic materials from both parents.

The most scientifically accurate description was provided by twelve-year-old Michael: "The sperm encounter one ovum, and one sperm breaks into the ovum which produces, the sperm makes like a cell, and the cell separates and divides. And so it's dividing, and the ovum goes through a tube and embeds itself in the wall of the, I think it's the fetus of the woman." It is the sophistication of this child's reasoning, not simply whether his explanation is correct, that indicates the level of his understanding. Michael's verbal error is like the error of an algebra student who understands quadratic equations but makes a mistake in multiplication.

Although other explanations for the necessity of the union of the reproductive cells are not as extensive, another defining quality of this level is the ability to coordinate the interplay of factors affecting reproduction — sex, love, religious teachings, and physiology — so that the role of each is kept distinct and then all are fitted together so that none overshadows or engulfs another.

Twelve-year-old Donna, asked how sexual intercourse starts a baby, answered from several angles: "Um, the fertilizing part, I guess. The part that a man and a woman love each other enough to have a child and to bring it into the world. If you want to think of the part that's the truth, or the mechanical stuff about it, the mother makes it. But if you were religious you think that God put it there, because He wants another child on the earth, and that your love sort of sends a message, telling Him that you want a child. And if you're little, you tell a kid that the stork brings it. I always figured that the stork was

God and He's putting the child there. I guess that's how the word that the stork brings it got around. But a woman can't have a baby without having sexual intercourse, because the man has organs in him that have to go or be put together with the woman's organs. If they're not put together, it's impossible."

Stage-Related Properties of the Origin of Babies Scale

So far, we have described a scale in which each new level represents inferences of increasing complexity (increasing differentiation and integration of the various aspects of conception and childbirth). We have also suggested that increasing proportions of the children in the older age groups gave higher levels of response (see Bernstein and Cowan, 1975, Table 2). There were other data to support the conclusion that ideas about babies emerge in cognitive stage sequence.

The children's responses to the Babies task were highly correlated with their responses to the other three Piagetian tasks — physical causality (origin of night), physical conservation (water), and social identity. Whole-sample correlations between pairs of tasks ranged from .73 to .83. In addition, there tended to be a correspondence between tasks in the absolute levels of responding; concrete operational performance in one task tended to be associated with the same level of performance in another.

Because data from all the tasks show similar developmental progression and because they are not only correlated but also tend to be associated in absolute level, it is reasonable to assume that the data reflect the operation of some underlying cognitive stage or structure. Of course, conclusive data concerning the necessary sequence of stages of ideas about babies can only come from longitudinal studies.

Children's Ideas About Sex and Sexuality

To an adult, it is obvious that an inquiry into the origin of babies must at some point deal with ideas about sex, sexual intercourse, and sexuality. Freud's discussion, briefly summarized at the beginning of this chapter, goes back and forth from inferences about children's ideas of conception to ideas about intercourse. Our data indicate that such links are generally absent in the responses of most young children in our sample. We are not saying here that young children are completely unaware of intercourse but rather that they appear to be unaware of its necessary role in reproduction. We acknowledge that our study focused on babies and that most of the data on sexuality were incidental to this focus. However, because we could not find any studies outside the psychoanalytic tradition that systematically examine children's thinking about sexuality, we believe that it may be helpful to convey some of our impressions based on the anecdotal data reported earlier.

While young children (Levels 1 and 2) do not connect the making of babies with male-female genital sexuality, a few do seem to be aware that there is a joint male-female role in the process. For example, children believe that the man or woman transfers the sperm to the egg with his or her hands. Interestingly enough, when some children at Level 3 and half the children at Level 4 do begin to refer to intercourse, with few exceptions they believe that it occurs only in connection with the intent to conceive a child. Furthermore, it seems to be a mysterious, complicated, and difficult act: Some children report that "a man and woman needed the doctor's help to perform such an operation." One youngster speculated that "it must have been a Saturday or Sunday for them to have the time to do it."

These descriptions portray an act remarkably devoid of sexuality in its affective or erotic sense. The association of intercourse with pleasure appears to be a relatively late development. In our study, it was rare for a child of eight to respond that parents have sexual intercourse because they love each other. Even by Level 6, only a few of the preteenagers volunteered that "liking the feeling of mating" or "for the pleasure of it—they enjoy it," may be sufficient motivation for genital sexuality.

In our qualitative data, it is only when the idea of sex for pleasure begins to emerge that some children are apparently forced to construct a theory of birth control. If parents do it more often than the few times required to have families of a particular size, children begin to speculate about factors that prevent conception. At first, they seem to believe that something about the way the act is done or when it is done stimulates conception. Also, younger children see marriage as some kind of necessary condition for conception to occur. Even when the children seem to have knowledge of the birth control pill, it is clear that there is no idea about how it works or its relation to the overall process of lovemaking and conception. Perhaps we will find a developmental sequence of theories about birth control, just as we have found a developmental sequence in children's ideas about other aspects of the reproductive process.

Cognitive and Emotional Development

In Freud's theory of psychosexual development, changes in the locus of sexual pleasure are the key definers of developmental stage (oral, anal, phallic, and so forth). Sexual development is considered primarily as an affective phenomenon, with biologically predetermined tendencies influencing the changes from one stage to the next. By contrast, in this chapter we have been emphasizing the cognitive-structural aspects of children's ideas about some of the topics involved in sexuality. We will attempt to deal with only two of the many complex issues involved in understanding the relation between these two realms.

One of us has provided a summary of Piaget's often sketchy discussions of the links between cognitive and affective development (Cowan, 1978). In brief, Piaget views the affective and cognitive aspects of development as inseparable and irreducible, with affectivity constituting the "energetics" of behavior patterns whose cognitive aspect refers to structure alone (Piaget and Inhelder, 1969, p. 20). Sometimes, in a manner similar to the psychoanalytic approach, he describes affect as an intrusion factor that promotes lower levels of cognitive performance in a given content area.

In our own study, this intrusion factor was often manifested as embarrassment, with some variations apparently attributable to age and stage. For the three-year-olds, embarrassment was minimal, although one child did say that she was shy about describing how the father puts the sperm in the egg. All of the seven-year-old boys at Level 1 in the Origin of Babies task showed signs of diffidence or embarrassment ranging from a terse "Don't know," to evasiveness, protestations of ignorance, and silliness. As a group, the seven-year-old boys revealed a lower level of reasoning about human reproduction than the seven-year-old girls: This was the only age at which statistically significant sex differences emerged. Perhaps the boys were in a latency phase characterized by a lack of interest in sexuality but an increased involvement in exploring their sex role. They certainly disclaimed any interest in babies, while many of the girls at that age had bedrooms replete with doll babies and playhouse furnishings.

From Level 4, as age and stage increased, forthrightness increased while the hesitance and giggling dropped off markedly. If these preliminary observations are supported by further research, we may be able to draw several important conclusions. First, there is little doubt that ideas about conception and babies have both cognitive and affective components. Second, the affective "energetics" may sometimes intrude so that they interfere with the child's ability to respond at the highest possible intellectual level. Third, there may be an interaction between the cognitive developmental level and the extent to which affective intrusions are disruptive.

Beyond the impact of affect on cognitive competence and performance, we are concerned with a more general issue in theories of sexual development. Freud assumed that powerful sexual instincts were operating in the child from the moment of birth and that anxieties could be triggered both by frustration of these instincts (that is, object loss) and by their satisfaction (that is, the acting out of Oedipal strivings). When we consider the fact that the theory of infantile sexuality began as a set of adult reconstructions and when, in addition, we consider our finding that there are consistent changes in interpretations of sexuality from childhood to adulthood, we arrive at a point where methodological and substantive issues overlap. Our data indicate that the connections between babies and sex and between sex and pleasure tend to emerge long after the Oedipal conflict is supposed to occur (ages four to five). To be sure, these are conscious reports and in themselves do not refute the possibility that the child's unconscious erotic impulses have been repressed. The question is how we, as adults, know about the child's sexuality. Does the sexual meaning of a behavior interpreted by the adult correspond with the meaning of this behavior to the child? Shouldn't we go beyond the notion that the locus of pleasure changes to consider the possibility that the nature of pleasure changes, from the child's point of view, as he or she moves to new levels of cognitive understanding?

The problem of the adult observer can be illustrated by one example of how parents interpret their children's behavior. Roberts, Kline, and Gagnon (1978), in their large survey of how sexuality is learned in the family, report that parents are usually relaxed about children touching their own genitals but that when the children reach a certain age (the case examples suggest around five or six) "self-exploration crosses some amorphous gray line to become 'masturbation,' with its erotic overtones" (p. 44). Does this shift represent a change in children or is it a change in attributions made by adults? The same question may be asked of therapists who depend heavily on sexual interpretations of children's play (as, for example, that trucks crashing together represent parental intercourse). The issue is not whether Freud's theory is right or wrong. The issue is that, before we make claims about the precise meaning and nature of childhood sexuality and its role in the general development of the child, we must interpret children's behavior more carefully.

Methodological Issues

One important problem in investigating children's thinking about reproduction and sexuality is the psychosocial context in which data gathering takes place. Parents and school personnel are often reluctant to cooperate with researchers wanting to investigate this topic. It is not every day that an adult sits down with a young child who is not his or her own to talk about birth and sexuality. On the one hand, it is the failure of open communication between adults and their own children that has led to this context of discomfort and to some of the nervous laughter shown by the children in our study. On the other hand, it is this same failure to communicate that makes this research so necessary. With a sensitive interviewer who is comfortable with the material and has a warm, yet matter of fact presentation, it is easy for most children to be comfortable and to relax after momentary embarrassment.

Given the sensitivity of the subject matter and the need to delve beneath the surface content to reach the child's idiosyncratic understanding and feelings, we strongly believe that the clinical interview as Piaget described it (1960a) is the method of choice for assessment of children's understanding of babies, birth, and sex. No cut and dried standardized test will do. Cowan (1978) describes the advantages of the clinical method in terms of a "triangulation" metaphor. The interviewer, situated at point B, and the child, situated at point C, discuss a set of events at point A. Using an extensive, unstandardized, yet systematic set of probes, the interviewer compares the child's view of the event (CA) with his or her own view (BA). Like the surveyor who triangulates a distant point by staking out two other observation points, the interviewer attempts to coordinate the differences in perspective between him or her and the child. In the process, the interviewer arrives at a better understanding of how the child interprets the stimulus (that is, to what question the child's response is an answer) and a better understanding of the response. The goal here is not the attainment of perfect objectivity, for that is impossible if one accepts Piaget's model of knowledge as an interactive construction by the observer. Instead, the goal is to provide a less egocentric interpretation of the system of interaction among the observer, the child, and the stimulus.

Beyond these general methodological cautions, it is important to mention one issue involved in scoring the protocols. The chief obstacle to classifying responses at different levels is the failure of the interviewer to obtain a sufficiently detailed interview with sufficient probes to elicit the child's thinking about the central variables. Level 1 is defined by the child's inability to go beyond where the baby is prior to birth to describe any prospect of conception. Levels 2 and 3 are distinguished by specific and diminishing forms of precausal distortions of the biological and social processes involved in human reproduction. Most critical is the child's set of responses to probes about how children start to grow and why the events described are both necessary and sufficient. This criterion alone serves to differentiate among Levels 4 through 6. Once coders are clear about the criteria, interrater reliability is quite high. In our own study it was 90 percent.

Education of Young Children

The central point in our discussion of stage-related issues is that children tend to assimilate information to their current level of understanding. The following is an example from an interview with a Level 2 child: To the question, "How would the lady get a baby to grow in her tummy?", the child responded, "Get a duck. 'Cause one day I saw a book about them, and they just get a duck or a goose and they get a little more growed and then they turn into a baby." When the interviewer went on to ask, "A duck will turn into a baby?", the child replied, "They give them some food, people food, and they grow like a baby. To get a baby, go to the store and buy a duck." When the interviewer then asked how the child had learned about this process, the child explained, "I just saw, find out from this book."

This story of the duck transformed into a baby highlights one of the difficulties children have with books that attempt to teach them about human reproduction by analogy with other animals. Often such books will start out with how other animals mate and give birth, working up the animal kingdom until they reach human beings. Using transductive reasoning, the Level 2 child assimilates several details into one process with no awareness that his or her version is any more fantastic than the correct version at the end of the book.

Many childhood misunderstandings of sex and reproduction are harmless and may sound charming. Other misconstrued realities may become lingering sources of worry. One six-and-one-half-year-old girl told her mother: "When I grow up, I'm not getting a daddy. And if I get a baby, I'm not going to let it out." Her belief that a baby could grow inside her body without her doing anything to set that process in motion leads to other upsetting thoughts. The idea of a baby inside who will never see the light of day, the feeling of being a reluctant mother turned jailor who must keep the baby locked within her body, must no doubt cause her a great deal of unhappiness. How relieved she would be to understand that if she didn't "get a daddy" no baby would begin to grow.

Another anecdote further illustrates how lack of understanding can produce symptoms and how discovering the distortion and providing remedial information can alleviate distress. A mother came to her three-year-old daughter's nursery school to consult with the teachers as to why her child had refused all food for five days. In talking with the child, whose mother was then pregnant, the teacher discovered that the little girl thought that she, too, had a baby in her tummy. By eating, the child went on to explain, she would be dumping "yukky" chewed food on the head of a baby. Recognizing that for many young children thinking of the baby as in the tummy leads to confusion between the digestive and the reproductive systems, the teacher explained that while it may appear that the baby is in the tummy, it is really in the uterus, near the stomach but separate from it, and it opens only to the vagina. Following this explanation, the child resumed eating.

Being aware of the ways in which children distort these biological processes can alert adults to sources of possible distress and the need for corrective information. The use of the words *seed* and *egg* for sperm and ovum are another source of potential confusion for young children who tend to take metaphors very literally. Swallowing seeds may create fear of pregnancy and eating eggs can foster images of cannibalism for those who, like the three-year-old who said to his mother, "If Daddy put his egg in you then I must be a chicken," cannot yet distinguish between ova and breakfast.

These examples are all chosen from normal children. In our view such examples represent almost inevitable misunderstandings, given the translation system through which young children filter incoming information. However, the examples are very similar to those used by child analysts (see, for example, Erikson, 1968) to describe neurotic anxieties in childhood. There are several alternative ways of interpreting this observation. Perhaps some of the responses made by children in therapy do not result from an essentially pathological process but are a normal outgrowth of their level of understanding. Or perhaps cognitive factors associated with developmental stages can *create* worries and preoccupations in children; in other words, cognitive factors can trigger emotional disturbance. It is also possible that emotional factors are important in determining why some children construct worrisome distortions while others appear to produce more charming and benign myths and legends. Again, we are left with a set of questions requiring further research.

Further study is also needed before we can speak knowledgeably about the best way to guide young children along the path from their present level to a more differentiated picture of human reproduction. Studies of moral development by Turiel (1969) and cognitive development by Kuhn (1972) provide a model for assessing the effects of educational materials on children of different levels of cognitive functioning. They suggest that concepts one level beyond the child's original stage of functioning will be assimilated, while prior stages will be rejected and later stages distorted or not comprehended. We expect that similar findings will be obtained in assessing the impact of educational materials about procreation. While this has not yet been empirically validated, one of us has written upon how using the next stage of reasoning about the origins of babies may be useful to parents in talking with their children about sex and birth (Bernstein, 1978).

A cognitive-developmental approach to this subject area in no way provides "a reason to encourage children in forming 'infantile' sexual concepts through offering them false or defective information," as is argued by Kreitler and Kreitler (1966, p. 377). Instead, it suggests that accurate information be provided in a manner geared to maximize the child's comprehension at each step along the developmental path. This means that sex education, like other forms of learning, cannot be done effectively in one sitting. As development proceeds, children will reevaluate and discard former misconceptions, organizing past learning to include present experience. Yesterday's answers give rise to tomorrow's questions. Thus, having a dialogue with a child is better suited to providing digestible information than a lecture which misses the opportunity to check out what he or she is understanding. A dialogue allows the adult to assess the foundation, ascertaining whether the explanation that follows will have adequate structural support.

Adolescence

Books and articles about sex education often focus on the need to acquaint younger children with the so-called facts of life. There is another area of sex education that is approaching the status of a national crisis; we need to address the issue of teenage pregnancies. While knowledge of contraception is only one factor in contraceptive use, it is still the case that more women of all ages who have more contraceptive knowledge use contraceptives more effectively (Goldsmith and others, 1972).*

Adults and adolescents who know about birth control do not always act on the basis of what they know, however; certain variables such as anxiety (Miller, 1973) and guilt (Goldsmith and others, 1972) may interfere with the decision of whether or not to use contraception.

In addition to the emotional variables that affect the teenage girl's use of contraception, cognitive-developmental factors may play a part in the gap between knowledge and action. First, it is important to acknowledge that some of the young men and women who participate in sexual activity do so because they actively want babies, though they are usually unable to anticipate what life with a baby will be like. This is true of men and women at every age (Cowan and others, 1978).

Cvetkovich and others (1975) speculate that the egocentric nature of adolescent thought, as described by Elkind (1967), contributes to a form of magical thinking in which wishing somehow makes it less possible to become pregnant. These authors imply that adolescents entering formal operations still have cognitive deficits that could lead to difficulties in making the connection between information and behavior. For example, from the fact that they "only did it a few times" and nothing happened, they conclude that they are not fertile.

---

*Like pregnancy and childbirth, contraceptive behavior is almost always investigated and discussed with an exclusive focus on women. We believe that this emphasis ignores the importance of the relationship context in which these events occur and specifically ignores the role of the male partner in the thinking and decision making about sexual activity, contraception, and pregnancy.

However, we would suggest that not all adolescents have the use of formal operations, especially in this emotionally loaded content area. Some sexually active adolescents probably resemble the preconceptual children we described earlier who do not yet connect sexual activity and pregnancy. Before designing new programs of sex education, we must find out much more about how these adolescents are assimilating the information that we are trying to provide. This very important practical problem may have one extremely important theoretical by-product. A study of the process of sex education and the match or mismatch between the course content and students' cognitive level would make it possible to find out a great deal more about the relation between cognitive understanding on the one hand and decision-making actions on the other.

Directions for Future Research

We have indicated issues and problems to which new studies must be addressed. A broader spectrum of the population, in terms of age, sex, and cultural range, is needed to validate the cognitive-developmental sequence we have described. Longitudinal study is needed to validate a necessary sequence of conceptual development in this area.

In the present chapter we focused on sexuality as an aspect of reproduction. But human sexuality is a more pervasive aspect of life than its reproductive function would imply and extends to sexual feelings and relationships that form the basis of family life, kinship structures, and social organization. We were unable to find a systematic study of children's cognition about sexuality. There are only a few sources that even begin to ask questions about the child's and adult's understanding of the relationship context in which sexuality develops and is expressed (Conn, 1947; Kreitler and Kreitler, 1966; Moore and Kendall, 1971).

We have defined sexual development in its broadest aspects as including intimacy, gender identity, gender roles, bodily function, erotic behavior, conception, reproduction, intercourse, and birth control. However, teaching in this area has been accompanied by an unfortunate tendency to investigate each topic separately. We need to take a more integrated look at how gender identity, gender role, sexuality, sexual preference, interpersonal intimacy, and psychological adjustment develop. We need to know not only how sexuality is viewed by adult researchers and clinicians but also how it is understood and experienced by children and adolescents themselves. Perhaps an attempt to integrate theory and research would have a corrective impact on our tendency to think about and to provide sex education in such a fragmented and isolated manner.

References

Bernstein, A. C. *The Flight of the Stork.* New York: Delacorte Press, 1978.

Bernstein, A. C., and Cowan, P. A. "Children's Concepts of How People Get Babies." *Child Development,* 1975, *46,* 77–91.

Breasted, M. *Oh, Sex Education!* New York: New American Library, 1971.

Conn, J. H. "Children's Awareness of the Origins of Babies." *Journal of Child Psychiatry,* 1947, *1,* 140–176.

Cowan, C., Cowan, P., Coie, J., and Coie, L. "Becoming a Family: The Impact of a First Child's Birth on the Couple's Relationship." In W. Miller and L. Newman (Eds.), *The First Child and Family Formation.* Chapel Hill: University of North Carolina Population Center, 1978.

Cowan, P. A. *Piaget with Feeling: Cognitive, Social, and Emotional Dimensions.* New York: Holt, Rinehart and Winston, 1978.

Cvetkovich, G., Grote, B., Bjorseth, A., and Sarkissian, J. "On the Psychology of Adolescents' Use of Contraceptives." *Journal of Sex Research,* 1975, *11,* 256–270.

Elkind, D. "Egocentrism in Adolescence." *Child Development,* 1967, *38,* 1025–1034.

Erikson, E. H. *Identity, Youth, and Crisis.* New York: Norton, 1968.

Freud, A. *Normality and Pathology in Childhood.* New York: International Universities Press, 1965.

Freud, S. "On the Sexual Theories of Children." In P. Rieff (Ed.), *The Collected Papers of Sigmund Freud.* New York: Collier, 1963. (Originally published 1908.)

Goldsmith, S., Gabrielson, M. O., Matthews, V., and Potts, S. "Teenagers, Sex, and Contraception." *Family Planning Perspectives,* 1972, *4,* 32–38.

Kreitler, H., and Kreitler, S. "Children's Concepts of Sexuality and Birth." *Child Development,* 1966, *37,* 363–378.

Kuhn, D. "Mechanisms of Change in the Development of Cognitive Structures." *Child Development,* 1972, *43,* 833–944.

Laurendeau, M., and Pinard, A. *Causal Thinking in the Child.* New York: International Universities Press, 1962.

Lemke, S. "Children's Identity Concepts." Unpublished doctoral dissertation, University of California, Berkeley, 1973.

Miller, W. "Sexual and Contraceptive Behavior in Young Unmarried Women." In D. Young and A. Erhart (Eds.), *Social, Cultural, and Behavioral Issues in Obstetrics and Gynecology.* New York: Plenum, 1973.

Moore, J. E., and Kendall, D. G. "Children's Concepts of Reproduction." *Journal of Sex Research,* 1971, *7,* 42–61.

Piaget, J. *The Child's Conception of the World.* Paterson, N.J.: Littlefield, Adams, 1960a. (Originally published 1929.)

Piaget, J. *The Child's Conception of Physical Causality.* Paterson, N.J.: Littlefield, Adams, 1960b. (Originally published 1930.)

Piaget, J. *On the Development of Memory and Identity.* Worcester, Mass.: Clark University Press, 1968.

Piaget, J., and Inhelder, B. *The Psychology of the Child.* New York: Basic Books, 1969.

Roberts, E. J., Kline, D., and Gagnon, J. "Family Life and Sexual Learning: A Study of the Role of Parents in the Sexual Learning of Children." Report of the Project on Human Sexual Development, Harvard University. Cambridge, Mass.: Population Education, Inc., 1978.

Turiel, E. "Developmental Processes in the Child's Moral Thinking." In P. Mussen, J. Langer, and M. Covington (Eds.), *Trends and Issues in Developmental Psychology.* New York: Holt, Rinehart and Winston, 1969.

Anne C. Bernstein is a clinical psychologist at the Rockridge Health Plan, Oakland, California.

Philip A. Cowan is professor of psychology and head of the psychology clinic at the University of California, Berkeley.

"Do you know why you got sick?" Children's ideas
about this and other aspects of illness follow
a developmental sequence.

Children's Conceptions of Illness

Roger Bibace
Mary E. Walsh

In psychological, psychiatric, and pediatric literature of the past several decades, there has been considerable attention given to the psychological needs of the ill child. Until very recently, the major theoretical format for understanding and intervening in the behavior of sick children has been psychoanalysis. A number of studies, both clinical and empirical, have addressed children's responses to illness and/or hospitalization in terms of the feelings of the child. The psychic and physical trauma experienced by the sick child were seen to result in feelings of fear, anger, anxiety, withdrawal, and depression. Thus, therapeutic interventions were best directed to the affective level— toward acknowledging and modifying these negative feelings.

But, even within the psychoanalytic orientation, it became obvious that the feelings of the sick child or adult were related to beliefs or concepts about illness—that is, to the way the patient understood illness at a cognitive level. For example, much of the depression and withdrawal of the hospitalized child was presumed to be related to the child's belief that he or she was being punished for wrongdoing or was to blame—was at fault—for the illness being contracted. The negative affect or feeling was in some way seen to be related to the child's cognition or understanding of the causes of the illness.

R. Bibace and M. Walsh (Eds.). *New Directions for Child Development: Childrens' Conceptions of Health, Illness, and Bodily Functions*, no. 14. San Francisco: Jossey-Bass, December 1981

This awareness among clinicians of the importance of the child's beliefs about illness, along with the academic psychologist's interest in cognition, has in the last two decades provoked a considerable amount of research about the child's concepts or ideas or illness. A number of different beliefs or concepts of illness have emerged in the research.

One of the early studies in this area confirmed the psychoanalytic interpretation that children believe that illness is a punishment for wrongdoing or that they are to blame for the illness. Brodie (1974), in a study of children, found this notion to be particularly prevalent among hospitalized children, but even among healthy children a full quarter of the sample thought that "boys and girls who misbehave get sick more often than those who are good" (p. 1157). More recently, Cook (1975) found this moral explanation to be characteristic only of the spontaneous accounts of illness offered by children. When children were challenged in a directive interview to explain to the best of their ability the cause of illness, the so-called moral explanation was far less frequent and under these circumstances occurred more frequently among sick than among healthy children.

But, in spite of the seeming predominance of this moral explanation, other beliefs, or concepts of illness, as they came to be called in the literature of cognitive development, have surfaced in the research. The belief that illness is caused by germs and/or contact with sick people was noted in several studies (Palmer and Lewis, 1975; Perrin and Gerrity, 1979). Being in the mere presence of a sick person was assumed by many children to be a potential cause of their becoming ill.

Palmer and Lewis (1975) observed in a number of children the concept of prevention — that is, the belief that illness can be avoided by certain activities of the person, for example, eating the appropriate foods or getting adequate rest.

A number of studies have pointed to a concept of illness in which psychological as well as physical processes are used to describe and/or explain the illness (Campbell, 1975; Natapoff, 1978; Palmer and Lewis, 1975).

An aspect of the child's belief system that has received considerable attention in the literature is the extent to which the child believes he or she is likely to get ill — that is, perceived vulnerability to illness (Gochman, 1971; Palmer and Lewis, 1975). Children have been found to differ from one another consistently in the degree to which they believe they will be victims of sickness or accidents.

Perceived vulnerability appears to be linked to another dimension of the belief system (Gochman, 1971) — locus of control — regarding the onset or healing of illness. Children differ from one another in terms of how much control they feel they can exert over events that cause or cure illness (Neuhauser and others, 1978).

In brief, the research of the past decade has demonstrated that the range of children's concepts about illness is broader than the original psychoanalytic notion that children understand illness predominantly in terms of punishment. Children also conceptualize illness in terms of catching germs, as an experience that they can avoid through certain behaviors, as having both psychological as well as physical aspects, and as an event to which they are to varying degrees vulnerable.

But as significant as the variety or range of explanations of illness offered by children is the order in which these explanations are manifest. The empirical evidence clearly suggests that the child's concept of illness changes in certain specifiable directions with age and/or development.

In contrast to those of the younger, immature child, the concepts of illness of the older, mature child evidence increased conceptual sophistication (Campbell, 1975), greater complexity (Natapoff, 1978; Perrin and Gerrity, 1979), more frequent reference to internal body cues (Natapoff, 1978; Neuhauser and others, 1978; Palmer and Lewis, 1975), more realism (Palmer and Lewis, 1975), more restricted definitions and focus (specificity) on specific diseases (Campbell, 1975), greater generalization based on principle (Perrin and Gerrity, 1979), greater differentiation and abstractness (Carandang and others, 1979; Simeonsson, Buckley, and Monson, 1979), greater integration of parts and wholes (Natapoff, 1978), more organized description of process and cause (Perrin and Gerrity, 1979), and increased number of categories to define health or cause of illness (Caradang and others, 1979; Natapoff, 1978).

It is evident from these studies that the child's conception of illness is clearly related to the child's developmental status. However, a number of situational variables have been found to affect the developmental level of the child's expressed concept. It has been demonstrated that the developmental level of the concept is related to the nature of the inquiry — that is, whether the interview is spontaneous, or structured (Cook, 1975), whether the disease under discussion is visible or invisible (Neuhauser and others, 1978), and the content of the question asked — for example, whether the question concerns the cause or cure of the illness or the function of medicine (Simeonsson, Buckley, and Monson, 1979). Surprisingly, there is no evidence to suggest that sex differences affect the concept of illness. Similarly, while effect on developmental level has not been the specific focus of several studies, they have shown that the influence of the mother's concept of illness has no significant effect on the child's concept (Campbell, 1975; Mechanic, 1964).

The data then converge around a single theme — that there are manifest age differences in the type of explanation of illness offered by children.

How have these age differences been interpreted in the literature? In general, studies have varied in the extent to which they integrate the empirical finding of age differences with theoretical explanations of development. A number of studies, predominantly early studies in this area, examine concepts of illness in children of differing ages with no reference to developmental theory. Such studies either categorize various explanations on themes offered by children and determine the frequency of each type of response at each age level or across all age levels (Brodie, 1974; Campbell, 1975; Mechanic, 1964); or dimensionalize an aspect of the child's explanation (for example, degree of perceived vulnerability to illness) and relate this dimension with age (Gochman, 1971). Only the empirical marker of age is utilized and no attempt is made to understand or explain age differences in terms of a theoretical framework, especially from the perspective of cognitive-developmental theory.

A second group of studies, done predominantly in or after the mid-seventies, address themselves specifically to examination of age-related changes in the concept of illness, but any explanation of these age changes in terms of cognitive-developmental theory occurs only in post hoc discussions of the findings. Thus we see, for example, Palmer and Lewis (1975) suggesting that young children's accounts of the cause of illness reflect "the syncretic thinking identified by Piaget" (p. 2), or Natapoff (1978) indicating that the quantitative and qualitative age-related changes in children's concept of health "are consistent with theories of concept development" (p. 995).

A third group of studies make much more explicit use of cognitive-developmental theory. Investigators in this group use developmental theory to make predictions about the types of differences in concepts to be expected at different ages (Campbell, 1975; Caradang and others, 1979; Neuhauser and others, 1978; Perrin and Gerrity, 1979; Simeonsson, Buckley, and Monson, 1979; Steward and Regalbuto, 1975). Usually, the differences consist of one or a few characteristics of the general and abstract developmental stages of Piaget (1930) or Werner (1948), such as global and undifferentiated thinking versus differentiated thinking, or magical thinking versus concrete logical thinking.

However, even though they specify the developmental dimensions along which the child's concept changes, none of these analyses of differences explicates the novel or unique way in which Piaget and Werner's general stages of cognitive development are expressed in the particular content area being investigated. Thus, these analyses provide no appreciation for the way in which the child assimilates a particular phenomenon or aspect of reality — that is, illness — to the general schemata that reflects the evolution of cognition. These studies merely reassert categories of the middle range — the existence of the general stages of cognitive development.

In our recent research (Bibace and Walsh, 1980), we spell out six qualitatively different categories of explanations of illness that are developmentally ordered. These categories are derived from a study of an initial sample of 180 children aged four to fourteen and validated in two subsequent studies (Bibace and Walsh, 1977, 1979). A description of these developmental categories of explanation of illness follows.

In general we derived three major types of explanations consonant with Piagetian stages of cognitive development: prelogical, concrete logical, and formal logical. Within each of these major categories we were further able to distinguish two subtypes of explanation. Thus, in addition to the category Incomprehension, which characterized a few of the very youngest subjects in our pilot study, we delineated six types of explanations of illness that were then developmentally ordered with chronological age used as the gross index of developmental status.

The categories are briefly described and illustrated below. (See Table 1 for tabular outline.)

The illustrations used refer to responses about a single type of illness — that is, a cold. The complete scoring system, available from the authors, provides numerous examples with regard to the range of illnesses sampled by the protocol.

Prelogical Explanations

According to Piaget (1930), prelogical thinking is typical of children between two and six years of age. It is characterized by children's inability to distance themselves from their environment and results in explanations accounting for the cause-effect relationship in terms of the immediate spatial and/or temporal cues that dominate their experience. In both types of prelogical explanations of illness — phenomenism and contagion — we see children being overly swayed by the immediacy of some aspects of their perceptual experiences.

Phenomenism represents the most developmentally immature explanation of illness. The cause of illness is an external concrete phenomenon that may co-occur with the illness but that is spatially and/or temporally remote. Children at

Table 1. Developmental Conceptions of Illness

I. *Prelogical Explanations*
Category 1: Phenomenism
Category 2: Contagion

II. *Concrete-Logical Explanations*
Category 3: Contamination
Category 4: Internalization

III. *Formal-Logical Explanations*
Category 5: Physiological
Category 6: Psychophysiological

---

this stage are unable to explain the manner in which these events cause the illness:

> How do people get colds? "From the sun." How does the sun give you a cold? "It just does, that's all."

> How do people get colds? "From trees."
> How do people get measles? "From God." How does God give people measles? "God does it in the sky."

Contagion is the most common explanation of illness offered by the more mature children in the prelogical stage. The cause of illness is located in objects or people that are proximate to, but not touching, the child. The link between the cause and the illness is accounted for only in terms of mere proximity or magic:

> How do people get colds? "From outside." How do they get them from outside? "They just do, that's all. They come when someone else gets near you." How? "I don't know — by magic I think." How do people get colds? "When someone else gets near them."

Concrete-Logical Explanations

Concrete-logical reasoning is manifest by children roughly between seven and ten years of age. In this stage, according to Piaget (1930), the major developmental shift is in accentuation of the differentiation between self and other, so that the child clearly distinguishes between what is internal and what is external to the self. This distinction is manifest in the two explanations of illness characteristic of this age group — contamination and internalization.

Contamination characterizes the explanations of younger children in the concrete-logical stage. The child now distinguishes between the cause of the illness and the manner in which it is effected. The cause is viewed as a person, object, or action that is external to the child and that has an aspect or quality that is bad or harmful for the body. Such a cause effects illness in the child either through the child's body physically contacting the person or object (for example, through touching, rubbing) or through the child's physically engaging in the harmful action and thus becoming contaminated:

> What is a cold? "It's like in the wintertime." How do people get them? "You're outside without a hat and you start sneezing. Your head would get cold, the cold would touch it, and then it would go all over your body."

Internalization is a type of illness explanation typically offered by older children in the concrete-logical stage. Illness is now located inside the body, while its ultimate cause may be external. The external cause, usually a person or object, is linked to the internal effect of illness through a process of internalization — for example, swallowing or inhaling. Even though the illness is now located within the body, it is described in only vague terms, evidencing confusion about internal organs and functions:

> What is a cold? "You sneeze a lot, you talk funny, and your nose is clogged up." How do people get colds? "In winter, they breathe in too much air into their nose, and it blocks up the nose." How does this cause colds? "The bacteria gets in by breathing. Then the lungs get too soft [child exhales], and it goes to the nose." How does it get better? "Hot fresh air, it gets in the nose and pushes the cold air back."

Formal-Logical Explanations

According to Piaget (1930), children who are approximately eleven years of age and older manifest formal-logical thinking. At this stage, there is the greatest amount of differentiation between the self and the other; conversely, the organism is least likely to manifest the effects of stimulus-boundedness because of the compensatory character of operational or logical thinking. In both the physiological and psychophysiological explanations of this stage, we note the greatest amount of differentiation between the external and internal world, so that the source of the illness is located within the body even though an external agent is often described as the ultimate cause.

Physiological explanations are usually offered by the younger children in the formal-logical stage. In this explanation, while the cause may be triggered by external events, the source and nature of the illness lie in specific internal physiological structures and functions. The cause is usually described as the nonfunctioning or malfunctioning of an internal organ or process, explained as a step by step internal sequence of events culminating in that illness:

> What is a cold? "It's when you get all stuffed up inside, your sinuses get filled up with mucus. Sometimes your lungs do too, and you get a cough." How do people get colds? "They come from viruses, I guess. Other people have the virus, and it gets into your blood stream and it causes a cold." Have you ever been sick? "Yes." What was wrong? "My platelet count was down." What's that? "In the blood stream they are like white blood cells. They help kill germs." Why did you get sick? "There were more germs than platelets. They killed the platelets off." How did you get sick? "From germs outside. They killed off the platelets."

Psychophysiological explanations represent the most mature understanding of illness. As in physiological explanations, the illness is described in terms of internal physiological processes, but the child now perceives an additional or alternative cause of illness—psychological cause. The child is aware that a person's thoughts or feeling can affect the way the body functions:

> What is a heart attack? "It's when your heart stops working right. Sometimes it's pumping too slow or too fast." How do people get a heart attack? "It can come from being all nerve-racked. You worry too much. The tension can affect your heart."

Consistent with the expectations of a cognitive-developmental framework, we found that the type of explanation of illness varied as a function of the developmental status of our subjects (see Table 2).

Among the four-year-olds, 54 percent gave contagion explanations and 38 percent contamination explanations. Among seven-year-olds, 63 percent gave contamination explanations and 29 percent internalization explanations. Among the eleven-year-olds, explanations were classified as 54 percent internalization and 34 percent physiological.

The findings of both the pilot study (Bibace and Walsh, 1977), with normal children from three to thirteen, and this study, with normal children aged four to eleven, were clearly congruent with the theoretical expectations regarding the qualitative differences in the cognitive processes relied upon by children. Further, the categories of responses, reflecting these qualitative differences in thinking, could be ordered in a developmental sequence consonant with the theoretical framework. Lastly, the frequency distributions of normal children who vary in chronological age are congruent with Piagetian theory and constitute empirical grounds for the value of those categories.

Table 2. Percentage of Subjects Manifesting Various Types of Explanations of Health and Illness

Type of Explanation	4 Years (N = 24)	7 Years (N = 24)	11 Years (N = 24)
0 Incomprehension	4		
1 Phenomenistic			
2 Contagion	54		
3 Contamination	38	63	4
4 Internalization	4	29	54
5 Physiological		8	34
6 Psychophysiological			8

As scientists relying on this theoretical perspective, we concluded what the earlier studies in this area (Cook, 1975) had already confirmed, that children's conceptions of illness reflect the more general processes (stages) of cognitive development as they have been articulated by Werner and Piaget. Thus, the preschooler's conception of illness as caused magically by clouds, or the sun, reflects the prelogical stage of cognitive development, in which cause and effect are linked by magical association. From the point of view of theoretical significance, therefore, our findings merely add to the list of studies that suggest that the child's concept of illness is related to his or her cognitive-developmental level.

The Scientific and Clinical Perspectives

These scientific findings and their utilization by clinicians, educators, and parents raise a number of more general issues. These include the different and complementary objectives of the scientist and the clinician. Another way in which this issue has been cast is the relative emphasis and valuation of forms, or the cognitive processes underlying thinking versus content, that is, what is being thought about. Scientists seek to arrive at generalizations that transcend contents and contexts. Clinicians require scientifically based generalizations that are applicable to specific contents and contexts. These issues are elaborated below.

Many studies relying on a developmental framework in the areas dealt with in this volume appear to have been initiated through an intuition or judgment that such studies were relevant to education, to patients, to the helping professions — that is, to individuals who were not merely interested in knowledge for its own sake. Rather, these audiences wanted to use such knowledge to help children, students, and patients. These differences in aim (the love of abstract knowledge for its own sake versus the utilization of knowledge in diverse settings, or the Kantian distinction between knowledge and judgment) have not been sufficiently acknowledged by many investigators. One purpose of this chapter is to argue that these different aims require more elaborate research strategies so that a classification system with a different end product (what we have called task-relevant categories) may evolve.

Our research accomplished what might be termed its scientific objective, confirmation of the validity of the general theory. The goal of the scientist is to articulate the universals — that is, the similarities among individuals — and to minimize individual differences. As our data demonstrate, general cognitive processes are indeed reflected in the specific contents of illness. Yet the conclusion that the child, dealing with health and illness contents, can also be shown to proceed through preoperational, concrete-operational, and formal-operational stages of causal reasoning would be completely unsatisfactory for clinicians. Those clinical-developmental psychologists who work with children and adults who are ill have an additional objective — to articulate a set of categories that are not only scientifically valid but also clinically useful. Whereas the scientist's search for universals leads to a focus on groups, the clinician focuses on the particulars — that is, the specific person. This is consonant with the clinician's goal of helping that person. For the scientist, the individuals in a group are the means to the end of attaining knowledge. For the clinician, general theoretical principles and findings must be specific to an individual if such theories or findings are to be helpful. The clinician therefore requires a classification system that simultaneously reflects the scientifically based general-formal categories of cognitive-developmental theory and the specific contents of the task. In order for developmental categories of the concept of illness to be useful to clinicians, the categories must reflect the relationship between health and illness questions and cognitive processes in a more intimate manner than research with the purely scientific objective of specifying the cognitive processes relied upon by the subject.

In much of the past research which has attempted to make cognitive-developmental psychology meaningful to clinicians, the difficulty of the relationship between form and content is clearly evident. The majority of these studies appear to have merely reiterated the formal-abstract categories. While such studies may have achieved their scientific objective, the findings are not very useful to clinicians who can better grasp and utilize the forms of organization inherent in the universals when they are concretized with respect to the contents which have relevance to both patient and therapist.

The categories that meet both scientific and clinical aims may be termed task-relevant categories. A methodological strategy that includes these categories is consonant with and exemplifies a central theoretical tenet of the type of theory that both Piaget and Werner espouse epistemologically. That is, both Piaget and Werner adhere to a genetic-interactionist position. Originally, we labeled such categories *categories of the middle range,* but that term has been used by sociologists to refer to categories solely derived from an inductive-empirical analysis of data. In contrast, we recognize explicitly that our categories are concretizations or particularizations of the abstract theoretical framework that we bring to the analysis of the data. Consequently, one could now view studies that merely reassert the validity of the abstract universals as being, from this interactional-theoretical position, reductionistic. They do not capture the specifics of the interaction between the subject and the particular task. Indeed, within a Piagetian framework, such studies reflect an imbalance between the assimilatory and accommodatory processes of the researcher. Here reductionism refers to the researcher's overemphasis on assimilating the subjects' products to an a priori abstract system of categories.

At the other end of the continuum are studies that focus solely on the content of the responses and do not probe the abstract universals or cognitive processes that such responses reflect. In contrast to studies that are reductionistic, this group of studies show the converse imbalance between the researcher's assimilatory and accommodatory processes. That is, the investigator can be criticized as overaccommodating to the specifics of the content of each experimental task. Typically, studies in this group present their findings in the form of tables that merely tabulate the frequency with which a particular content has been verbalized. There is no assimilation of these diverse contents to some more general abstract schema that can be applied consistently to other contents.

Methods and Procedures for Elaborating
Task-Related Categories

The process through which we articulated the task-relevant categories with respect to illness provides an illustration of the ongoing dialogue between theory and data. Our beginning point was theory—specifically, the hypothesis that the seemingly infinite variety of explanations of illness could be subsumed by a limited range of categories and that these categories could be developmentally ordered in a manner that reflected both the sequence and structure of the major stages of cognitive development (Piaget, 1930; Werner, 1948).

If one focuses solely on the formal or abstract level, the categories—that is, Piaget's abstract stages of cognitive development—have already been generated and one need only confirm or disconfirm their existence in concrete data. The child's responses are then analyzed in terms of the presence or absence of the characteristics of the different stages—for example, magical thinking in the preoperational stage or hypothetical thinking in the formal-operational stage.

Consistent with our expectation, we initially examined the concepts or explanations of illness offered by subjects representing the entire range of cognitive development. In order to insure subjects representing each of the major stages of cognitive development, we selected children—subjects from a population where cognitive development is most clearly evident. Further, in order to maximize the possibility that there might be explanations offered that would not be covered by the category system, we selected subjects from each and every age along the entire continuum of cognitive development.

This sample of explanations were ordered initially using the criterion of age—youngest to oldest. However, at this point in the theory-data dialogue (that is, in the balance between the assimilatory and accommodatory schemas of the investigators), age was subordinated to sequence and order. Within the ordered data, all the various forms of explanation were categorized empirically according to the most salient feature of content, as, for example, explanations that attributed the cause of illness to a remote external person or object: "A cold is from the sky"; "God gives you a stomach ache." Each of the types or forms of explanation that emerged were more clearly evident in one broad age group rather than another. In addition, the general or overall order provided by age was congruent with a developmental sequence within which these various explanations emerge. However, it is crucial to note that age could not in any way be rigidly adhered to as the sole developmental marker, since it was possible, for example, that the explanation of illness offered by a single normal six- or seven-year-old was more characteristic of that offered by most four-year-olds. On the other hand, age could be used as a general index of development; for example, no normal twelve-year-old offered explanations characteristic of the four-year-old modal response and vice versa. Thus, while age and stage were not seen, either from a theoretical or an empirical perspective, to be equivalent, they were strongly correlated during the early phases of ontogenesis for normal children.

In spite of the clear argument that can be made for using age as a developmental indicator, there are many who would challenge this assumption, arguing instead for an independent index of developmental status, in particular, a measure of performance on such other cognitive tasks as conservation of weight, causal reasoning regarding the origin of night, and perspective-taking tasks (Perrin and Gerrity, 19979; Simeonsson, Buckley, and Monson, 1979).

It seems to us, however, that there is no index that is, in the real sense of the word, independent. All are embedded in content, and there is abundant evidence that content strongly affects the form of thought — or cognitive stage (Walsh, 1974). Further, we would suggest that the index least embedded in content is age, and as long as one assumes that it is not equivalent to stage but, rather, only correlated with stage, as abundant evidence suggests, then age is an appropriate index of developmental status (Wohlwill, 1973). Age and stage are strongly correlated for normal children up to about thirteen, but the relationship between age and stage is clearly not correlated, in that the six categories do appear to be exhaustive for all people at all ages. Old people, for instance, are distributed among categories that are not among the most mature.

While the theoretical issue of cognitive stage or structure of thought was a central concern in our study, the categories themselves were articulated in terms of content as well as structure or form. Thus we described a category typical of the youngest children, in which "illness is described in terms of concrete perceptual events with no reference to the inside of the body or even to the body itself. The cause of illness is seen to be remote external objects or persons and the link between the cause and the illness itself can only be explained in terms of magic." In spite of the predominance of content in this example, the underlying structure of the thought can be discerned, the concrete perceptual-magical thinking characteristic of the preoperational stage of cognitive development. It is this focus on the integration of form and content that requires that the cognitive maturity of the response be the overriding criterion for scoring rather than the presence or absence of the so-called correct answer. Piaget consistently argued against the use of *wrong/right* as a way to classify children's thought.

Once the initial set of categories (six in our case) had been generated, an independent sample of children representing the three major stages was used to validate them. Here again, age was used as the developmental indicator. Our study also showed this grouping of responses in terms of these three age groups: Evidence from innumerable studies had suggested that preoperational thinking is characteristic of most children between three and six, concrete-operational thinking is characteristic of children between seven and ten, and formal-operational thinking is characteristic of children eleven and older. This widely accepted finding supported our selecting four-, seven-, and eleven-year-olds as the age groups that would represent each of the major stages.

The major hypothesis of the validation study was that the type of explanation of illness would vary as a function of the developmental status of the subjects, that explanations emerging earlier in the posited developmental sequences would be more typical of the younger subjects, while most of the older subjects would offer explanations that emerge later in their developmental sequence.

While the categories must clearly reflect the particulars of the content, clinical usefulness argues for some degree of generality so that the clinician will not be required to keep in mind a large number of specific category systems. Consequently, the categories we developed encompassed illness in general and not merely specific illnesses (such as, cold) as was done in some of the earlier studies (Cook, 1975). This kind of clinically oriented research requires that investigators decide on the range of contents and hence the generality of the concepts to be studied. The categories to be articulated in a study must clearly reflect the particulars of the contents and still allow for clinically meaningful generalization. Thus our study investigated specific illnesses such as colds, heart attacks, and so on. However, the inquiry into these specific contents was aimed at articulating the child's general conceptions of illness at the same developmental level across a variety of contents. Piaget described what he termed horizontal decalage—that is, consistently different rates of development across such content areas as conservation of mass, weight, volume (Flavell, 1963). Give the variability across different contents, how does one determine a single stage or category that is most appropriately characteristic of the child? When assessing cognitive development, some investigators (Perrin and

Gerrity, 1979) rely on the mean or average score, or developmental category, across a range of contents. Other investigators (Damon, 1977) have argued that the child's level of cognitive development is best described as the highest level of thinking the child consistently manifests. As an empirical measure we have opted for the latter approach and have characterized a subject by the highest category, or level of thinking, at which the subject responds two or more times (consistently).

While some of the variability in level of reasoning across contents can be attributed to varying rates of cognitive development, it is essential to examine the data for any other sources of systematic variation that consistently yield a lower or higher level of response. In the literature on developmental concepts of illness, a number of variables have been systematically examined: the perceptual aspects of the stimulus, the degree of familiarity of the stimulus, mode of presenting the task, and the affective status of the subject.

The perceptual characteristics of the illness result in a systematic variation in response. Illness that can be seen, such as a skin rash, in contrast to illnesses that cannot be seen, such as a stomach ache, facilitate a higher level of causal reasoning (Neuhauser and others, 1978).

The degree of familiarity of the stimulus — in this instance, the type of illness — has an effect on the level at which the child conceptualizes the illness. For example, the conceptualization of some common illnesses such as colds have apparently no developmental trajectory. Simeonsson, Buckley, and Monson (1979) report that subjects at various cognitive stages of development have similar conceptions of a cold. However, Piaget's theory, substantiated by empirical work in a number of domains, in addition to our findings in this content area, would suggest that sufficient probing would reveal the expected differences. For instance, we found repeatedly that, while initial responses often appeared very similar and even identical across the age groups, further probing revealed significant differences in the quality of reasoning underlying the responses.

Researchers, for the past four or five decades, have also speculated and studied whether the type or mode of presentation of the question to the subject (for example, verbal versus pictorial) might affect the level of the response. In an analysis of this issue with respect to illness, Simeonsson, Buckley, and Monson (1979), in keeping with previous findings, found no differences in response between pictorial and verbal modes of presentation.

Still other investigators have questioned whether how the question is asked would affect the child's level of causal reasoning. For instance, Cook (1975), in examining how children respond to spontaneous versus structured modes of questioning, found a consistently higher level of responses for the structured mode of questioning. However, this finding may be due to the higher levels of reasoning that emerge when a child's spontaneous utterances are sufficiently probed. Indeed, this is why Piaget insisted on the use of what he called the clinical method of inquiry, since the spontaneous or initial response may very well not be representative of that child's cognitive level of development.

Another variable presumed to affect the way in which a person thinks about illness is the affective or emotional states of the subject. Brodie (1974), for example, found that anxiety was related to the way in which the child reasoned about illness. The more fundamental issue here from the perspective of developmental psychology is the interrelationship between cognitive and affective processes. Both theoretical conceptualizations and empirical findings have dwelt on the question as to whether or not affective states accelerate or delay cognitive development. But the explanations of many such studies remain ambiguous. If affective variables accelerate the rate of cognitive development, then it can be argued that familiarity with one's illness enhances the level of understanding. If, however, the rate of cognitive development appears to be decelerated when certain affective states are present, it can be argued that the experience of illness has such overwhelming emotional concomitants that the level of conceptualization with respect to the illness is inhibited or regressed. Relying on current cognitive-developmental theories apparently limits the range of relationships that can be posited between cognitive processes and affective states. Outcome measures in such terms as the acceleration or delay of development focus only on the rate of development. They do not speak to the qualitative aspects involved in the organization of cognitive and affective factors: how these factors develop, and how they are related to one another under different affective conditions or at different stages of cognitive development.

Clinical Implications

How can these findings be used? We will describe three significant uses. An appreciation of the patient's conceptions of illness (1) fosters empathy; (2) facilitates explanation of illness and medical procedures; and (3) bolsters health education.

These general categories of meaning are useful clinically because, insofar as we zero in on the patient's meaning for his or her illness, we can foster empathy with the patient. And, of course, this sort of understanding could have all sorts of implications for the health professional in terms of where to go and how to get there. Helping patients to feel that their ideas about themselves and their illness are understood, not weird, contributes to workable and rewarding health professional–patient relationships.

The utilization of this category system by health professionals can assist relatives and other staff in dealing with patients who are ill. Fears that the professional may consider irrational can become more understandable through a developmental analysis of the patient's conceptions of illness. Such interpretations can have direct implications for better patient management. We have seen, for example, many five- or six-year-old children on a hospital pediatric unit become inexplicably upset and ask to be moved to another room. Their fears were based on their preoccupation with catching the disease of their roommate. It should be helpful for a health professional to appreciate that this is normal for children or immature adults in the *contagion* stage of cognitive development. Such an appreciation will prevent the health professional from dismissing such fears as irrational and will allay the frustration caused by the patient's lack of understanding. Even if the health professional is unable to make physical changes to alleviate the patient's worry, he or she can at least accept and not dismiss the patient's fear and hence offer genuine reassurance. Further, the health professional can better explain the reason for the patient's upset to the other staff members. Such explanations or remedial actions should increase the patient's sense of control. Patients' fear that they are at the mercy of the diseases they perceive around them can be directly acknowledged and addressed.

In recent years, there has been an enormous emphasis on the importance of communication in the health professional–patient relationship, particularly in the realm of patient education. Doctors and other health professionals are taught to respect patients' requests for an explanation of their illness. But often their intuitive attempts to respond to these requests lead them to rely on scientific explanations, or what we would call *physiological* explanations. The patient's inability to grasp these explanations can lead to the doctor's frustration. Our data will hopefully increase the kind of alternative explanations that doctors can rely on in their attempts to communicate with patients. For instance, our studies (Bibace and Walsh, 1980) show a large number of elderly patients in the category of *internalization*. This would suggest that a concrete analogy might be more effective in explaining a particular illness to some elderly patients than an abstract physiological one. However, even though the largest number of elderly are in this category, it should be remembered that it is important to find out first how the individual patient relates to his or her illness. Determining the particular category of explanation suitable for a particular individual will be less of a problem for family physicians who, through continuity of care, come to know their patients (Stephens, 1975). Providing alternative explanations should also be easier for family physicians, who have the opportunity to deal with people throughout the life cycle.

Live patient education efforts might also incorporate these cognitive-developmental differences in people's understanding of illness. For instance, preoperative teaching with a five-year-old would focus primarily on external observable events surrounding the surgery, such as the light in the operating room, uniforms of nurses, and so forth. This would be consistent with the young child's experience of illness in terms of external observable events. However, preoperative teaching about the same event with an older child who is at the abstract-logical stage of cognitive development would focus on the details of anatomy — what would be happening to the inside of his or her body. This is consistent with the child in the *physiological* category, who can conceptualize internal parts of the body as well as their functioning.

We have just suggested some answers to the question we are most often asked by clinicians: "How can I use these findings with patients?" But there is another aspect of this approach that we would like to stress because it is what originally got us interested in this research. We are intrigued, fascinated, and invigorated by what children and adults tell us regarding their ideas about how the body functions. And, for some of the health professionals with whom we work our finding that all ideas about illness follow a developmental sequence is not only of empirical interest but also has significant clinical import.

References

Bibace, R., and Walsh, M. E. "The Development of Children's Concepts of Health, Illness, and Medical Procedures." Paper presented at the Annual Meeting of the American Psychological Association, San Francisco, August 26, 1977.

Bibace, R., and Walsh, M. E. "Developmental Stages of Children's Conceptions of Illness." In G. Stone, F. Cohen, and N. Adler (Eds.), *Health Psychology: A Handbook.* San Francisco: Jossey-Bass, 1979.

Bibace, R., and Walsh, M. E. "Development of Children's Concepts of Illness." *Pediatrics,* 1980, *66* (6), 912–917.

Brodie, B. "Views of Healthy Children Toward Illness." *American Journal of Public Health,* 1971, *64* (12), 1156–1159.

Campbell, J. D. "Illness Is a Point of View: The Development of Children's Concepts of Illness." *Child Development,* 1975, *46* (1), 92–100.

Carandang, M., Folkins, C., Hines, P., and Steward, M. "The Role of Cognitive Level and Sibling Illness." *American Journal of Orthopsychiatry,* 1979, *49* (3), 474–481.

Cook, S. D. "The Development of Causal Thinking with Regard to Physical Illness Among French Children." Unpublished doctoral dissertation, University of Kansas, 1975.

Damon, W. *The Social World of the Child.* San Francisco: Jossey-Bass, 1977.

Flavell, J. H. *The Developmental Psychology of Jean Piaget.* Princeton, N.J.: D. Van Nostrand, 1963.

Gochman, D. "Some Correlates of Children's Health Beliefs and Potential Health Behavior." *Journal of Health and Social Behavior,* 1971, *12* (2), 148–154.

Mechanic, D. "The Influence of Mothers on Children's Health Attitudes and Behavior." *Pediatrics,* 1964, *33* (3), 444–453.

Natapoff, J. N. "Children's Views of Health: A Developmental Study." *American Journal of Public Health,* 1978, *68* (10), 995-1000.

Neuhauser, C., Amsterdam, B., Hines, P., and Steward, M. "Children's Concepts of Healing: Cognitive Development and Locus of Control Factors." *American Journal of Orthopsychiatry,* 1978, *48* (2), 335-341.

Palmer, B. B., and Lewis, C. E. "Development of Health Attitudes and Behaviors." Paper presented at the American School Health Association Convention, Denver, October 9-12, 1975.

Perrin, E. C., and Gerrity, P. S. "The Development of Concepts Regarding Illness." Paper presented at the 19th Annual Meeting of the Ambulatory Pediatric Association, Atlanta, May 1, 1979.

Piaget, J. *The Child's Conception of Physical Causality.* London: Kegan Paul, 1930.

Simeonsson, R. J., Buckley, L., and Monson, L. "Conceptions of Illness Causality in Hospitalized Children." *Journal of Pediatric Psychology,* 1979, *4* (1), 77-84.

Stephens, G. "The Intellectual Basis of Family Practice." *Journal of Family Practice,* 1975, *2* (6), 423-428.

Steward, M., and Regalbuto, B. A. "Do Doctors Know What Children Know?" *American Journal of Orthopsychiatry,* 1975, *45* (1), 146-149.

Walsh, M. E. "A Developmental Analysis of the Relationship Between Perceptual and Representational Processes." Unpublished doctoral dissertation, Clark University, 1974.

Werner, H. *Comparative Psychology of Mental Development.* New York: Science Editions, 1948.

Wohlwill, J. F. *The Study of Behavioral Development.* New York: Academic Press, 1973.

Roger Bibace is professor of psychology at Clark University and adjunct professor in the Department of Family and Community Medicine, University of Massachusetts Medical Center, Worcester.

Mary E. Walsh is associate professor of psychology at Regis College and an adjunct associate professor in the Department of Family and Community Medicine, University of Massachusetts Medical Center, Worcester.

*Young children's conceptions of internal body organs and their functions
are often both surprisingly accurate and surprisingly limited.
This chapter demonstrates children's developmental progress
toward more sophisticated conceptions.*

Children's Conceptions of
the Body Interior

Cathleen Crider

Most of us, if we think back to the time when we were seven or eight, can recall
the confusion we experienced when we first heard that the human heart was
not really shaped like a heart. Perhaps, too, you can recall a time when you cut
yourself and, seeing the blood flow out, wondered where it was coming from
inside your body. Perhaps you heard an exasperated mother exclaim, "The
way he eats, I'd swear he had a hollow leg!" More than once you probably
heard a parent or teacher command you to use your brain. And like any child—
or any good scientist for that matter—you drew on all the data at hand, all that
you had seen and felt and heard said, and you made up a story about your
body. When you were seven, perhaps it went something like this one: "Your
heart is this roundish thing in your chest that goes beep, bump, bump, like a
drum. It goes faster when you run. When your heart pumps it's so you can
breathe. When you eat, you have to go to the bathroom."

As you grew older, you added more data and rewrote your story in
ever more sophisticated ways. You gave the roundish thing in your chest a
more exact shape, with chambers and valves, and you were able to explain
that the drumbeat is neurally regulated. You began to understand that between
eating and going to the bathroom there is a whole sequence of physiological
transformations involving several body systems.

R. Bibace and M. Walsh (Eds.). *New Directions for Child Development: Childrens' Conceptions of Health,
Illness, and Bodily Functions*, no. 14. San Francisco: Jossey-Bass, December 1981

But how exactly does the young child build his or her first story? Then, through what sequence does that story get elaborated into a scientifically accurate account? How does the child who once thought in very simple ways arrive at fancy physiological explanations? Such are the questions that guide this chapter.

The State of a Young Child's Knowledge

According to the existing literature on conceptions of the body interior, the typical grade school child, when asked about the contents of the body, is likely to identify the brain, bones, heart, blood, and blood vessels (Gellert, 1962; Porter, 1974; Schilder and Wechsler, 1935; Smith, 1977; Tait and Ascher, 1955). At the age of ten or eleven, he or she would probably add the stomach to his or her list. As the child grows even older, the list starts to include lungs, muscles, nerves, kidneys, intestines, and other major organs (Gellert, 1962; Porter, 1974).

While omitting the stomach in their accounts, younger children often do include nonorgans, such as food and blood, and noninternal parts, such as the skin and belly button. Why this selection of contents? Surely every five-year-old has heard of the stomach and could point to its location. Schilder and Wechsler (1935) have suggested that, in the child's mind, the only thing he or she can be certain the body contains is what has been put into it. Thus, "even if he [or she] has heard of the stomach, it is unimportant in comparison with its contents" (p. 359). This appears to be the case with the seven-year-old whose drawing is reproduced in this chapter (see Figure 1). Although when asked about the stomach, she said, "It's a round thing your food goes inside," in her spontaneous drawing she included only the food. Furthermore, she stated that the food we eat goes "into the stomach, down to the leg, then to the little toe, then it stays in the toe." While this last remark appears somewhat playful, an example of what Piaget calls *romancing,* it nevertheless suggests the notion that, if there is anything at all in your leg and toe, it must be the food you eat.

This child's drawing is also notable for its inclusion of both internal and external parts in the same drawing. As Nagy (1953) has documented, the typical young child (roughly, the child under eleven years) does not consistently distinguish internal from external functions. Organs tend to be represented as nonspecific, roundish closed figures, said to be made of bones, skin, blood, and flesh or food. Each organ is given a single static function—for example, the brain is for thinking and the lungs are for air. The child is not able to explain this function in terms of a transformation, such as is involved in gas exchange. Neither is the child able to recognize such complementary functions as incorporation of food and elimination of waste. The child simply draws a

Figure 1. Drawing of Body Interior by Seven-Year-Old Girl

one-to-one correspondence between organ and function. In addition, the egocentric, concrete features that have often been shown to characterize childish thinking in other contexts are evident here. The literature contains many charming examples, including one child's assertion that "the appendix is just like Kleenex, made of tissue" (Gellert, 1962, p. 314).

While Nagy has clearly summarized the general characteristics of young children's notions of organ function, there is in fact a good deal of variation in the specific ideas children entertain. There is no one typical idea of heart function, no one typical idea of what lungs are for. Children's various ideas about heart function, as classified by Gellert (1962, pp. 332–333) are listed below, in order to show the range of concepts children use. The responses are ordered from those given primarily or exclusively by younger children to those mentioned most consistently by older children.

1. Don't know.
2. Function related to emotional processes — for example, to love.
3. Function related to health — for example, to keep you well.
4. Function related to superego — for example, to make you do the things you should.
5. Description of heart sound — for example, ticks.
6. Description of heart action — for example, thumps, beats, pumps.
7. Heart is essential to life.
8. Function related to breathing.
9. Function related to being able to move the body or supply energy.
10. Description of variation in heart rate or speed — for example, goes fast when you run.
11. Function related to blood, without concept of circulation — for example, blood comes from the heart.
12. Function related to purification and/or renewal of body parts or content.
13. Heart is essential to life explained in terms of circulation, blood, or oxygen.
14. Heart pumps blood, makes it circulate.

The data on what children think about the body interior have been clearly documented, especially by Nagy (1953) and Gellert. However, these data remain relatively unarticulated theoretically. How do we interpret the findings? In what way does the young child's conception, for all its idiosyncrasy and charming concreteness, constitute a reasonable and adaptive story about the inside of the body? How does the child get from an explanation of heart function in terms of love and health to an explanation of its role in the circulation of blood? How is it that children are consistently able to identify some organs before others? How is it that the child comes to distinguish organs from nonorgans and to give up his or her notion that food is the most important thing inside the body? What is the relationship between a child's knowledge of body parts and his or her understanding of functions?

In order to answer these questions, I have formulated a series of developmental levels in the conception of the body interior, based on observational data and a specific developmental theory. The primary data used in the formulation of these levels are verbatim records from structured interviews of twenty-one children aged six through twelve. Each child was first asked to tell what is inside the body, to draw it, and to locate various organs on a schematic drawing provided by the examiner. Then the child was asked to answer a series of questions about the constitution and function of the heart, lungs, stomach, intestines, brain, skin, and muscles. The child was also questioned about what happens to the food we eat and the air we breathe. In addition to this raw data, the developmental sequence draws to some extent on Gellert's categories for conceptions of specific organ functions.

My conceptual and methodological base can be found in the developmental theories of Werner (1947) and Piaget (1929, 1958). From Werner, I take my basic definition of development: "Wherever development occurs, it proceeds from a state of relative globality and lack of differentiation to a state of increasing differentiation and hierarchic integration" (1947, p. 126). It follows from this definition that conceptualizing development is in good part a logical project. It begins with an analysis of the hierarchical organization implicit in mature forms of thought and behavior. In the present context, we ask what distinctions and subsequent integrations are necessary in order to think about the body interior in our own sophisticated adult ways. Then we must construct logically, following Werner's orthogenetic principle, the order in which these distinctions and integrations must occur.

Piaget's stages of operational thinking constitute a formal developmental series consistent with Werner's principles and grounded in careful observation of what children say and do. Thus they offer a rough outline of the progression we might expect in thinking about the body interior. Specifically, the initial (preoperational) conceptions of body functions should deal with relatively global states of the whole body as immediately perceived, without clear differentiation of internal and external. Functions should be conceived in terms of purposes or final causes and relationships in terms of spatial and temporal contiguity. At a somewhat higher level (concrete-operational) a variety of structures and functions should be clearly differentiated. The conception of functions should be in terms of coordinated movements in space and time, relating different perceived states to one another. Higher level, more integrated (formal-operational) conceptions should posit hypothetical transformations that account for the perceived functioning of the body. Functions should be hierarchically organized in terms of organs, systems, and the interdependencies of systems.

The following discussion of levels of conceptualization of the body interior is an attempt to organize what children actually say about their bodies in terms of this abstract developmental outline.

Levels of Conceptualization

Suppose we could follow one ideal child (a girl, for the sake of ease in pronouns) as her thinking progresses across the levels of conceptualization. The progression might look something like what follows:

The child's first conceptualization of her body focuses on global and observable activities, without any differentiation of structure and function.

She might say, for example, "You breathe." She does not know what happens to the air we breathe in and may not even think to ask this question. Neither does she know of any interior organ that corresponds to this organismic activity. When asked about lungs, she replies, "I don't know what lungs are; I never saw one."

At the same time, the child begins to recognize certain parts of the body, differentiated by their spatial locations, such as the stomach, bones, and "muscles in your arm." At first they exist simply as parts of the body geography. The child does not yet even wonder what bones and muscles are for or how they work.

Our ideal child, by the age of six or seven years, is able to name a few organs and to talk about their functions, although still in only partially differentiated fashion. "Your heart," she says, "is for love. If you didn't have a heart, you wouldn't be alive." As for the brain, she explains that it is "part of the head." What is it for? "It's to think with; helps you to work or to play." How does it work? "You think of something. There's something in here that reminds you." At this level, body functions are still described in terms of perceived activities and states (working, playing, being alive). Each organ is defined as the origin or center of one of these functions. It is not yet understood to be the agent or a differentiated action but is rather treated as the first or final cause of a global function. The heart is for love.

The next step in our child's understanding of her body entails a specification of the nature of an organ in terms of its perceptual attributes, its shape, substance, or characteristic motion. "The heart is something that pumps inside the body." Such an organ can now be more specifically related to body activities by a similarity of superficial attributes and/or contiguity in space and time. When asked what the heart is for, she replies, "It helps you move around, so you will be living." How does it work? "When you breathe it pumps." The differentiation is still only partial. All forms of body motion are assimilated to one another, because of their perceptual similarity.

Further development occurs when structure and function are clearly differentiated and are related to one another in terms of a third factor—the movements of tangible body substances. "The stomach," our child now says, "is a round thing in our body for holding food. The food goes in your mouth, down your neck, to your stomach. If we didn't have a stomach the food would go everywhere and it would be a mess." Similarly, "Lungs are tubes down your throat. They go to your heart and stomach. You breathe by them." At this level, functions are conceived in terms of the spatial displacement of body substances. The organ continues to be conceived as the locus of a function but is further described as a container or a station in a sequence of displacement.

Even the brain is described in the language of spatial containers. "When you say something, it goes to your brain and you remember it."

Once the child comprehends spatial displacements, a new understanding of organs as active agencies becomes possible: The organ is what causes the displacement of body substances or parts. The motion of an organ that may earlier have been identified perceptually is now treated as the cause of a specific displacement. The heart is not only something that pumps inside your body, but more specifically, it "pumps blood out into your vessels and it goes through your body." So too, "muscles are something in your leg to help you bend; when you bend your leg, that's your muscle working." Thus there is a new coordination of structure and function.

At the next level of conceptualization, there is further differentiation within the movements of organs and substances, and they are treated as coordinated or reversible. The heart takes on two distinct and coordinated pumping jobs. "One side of your heart pumps blood in; the other side pumps it out." Similarly, "When you breathe, your lungs are taking air in and sending it back out." It is the stomach, however, that is often conceptualized first in terms of a complex system of coordinated movements. The child says, "Your stomach gathers the food you eat. It uses some of it and gets rid of waste." What happens to the food we use? "It goes into the veins, goes to your cells," while the waste "comes out when you go to the bathroom."

Still further development occurs when the transformation of specific body substances is conceived of. Transformations are initially identified by their beginning and end points: One body substance becomes another. "When we eat it goes to the stomach and gets all mashed up. Then it's liquid, it's blood, and it goes into your legs and arms." The process may be further described by analogy to processes observed in the external perceptual world. Structures may be defined somewhat animistically as the agents of transformation: "There's blood and something in the stomach that eats up food, makes it turn into blood and water." The transformation may even be given a moral status. "Lungs purify air. You breathe in good air and breathe out bad air."

Finally, when levels of body organization are differentiated and transformations are conceived as coordinated or reversible, physiological explanations become possible. Phenomenal transformations are explained by shifting the analysis from the level of organs and substances to the level of cells and chemical reactions. Body processes are characterized by continuous cycles of assimilation, breakdown, and/or exchange. Organs are internally differentiated in a manner corresponding to their transforming systems. Thus, at thirteen years, our ideal child says, "You breathe in oxygen and let out carbon dioxide. Oxygen goes to the lungs and is diffused into the blood stream. The lungs have little air sacs with capillaries in them, where oxygen diffuses into the blood. It goes into your cells. Then it comes back out as carbon dioxide." The child can explain, too, how the heart plays a role in this process. "The heart pumps blood all around the body and then it comes back. Blood gives off oxygen and stuff, and then it goes back to the heart for more."

There are of course some gaps and slight inaccuracies in this thirteen-year-old's idea of respiration and circulation. What is more important, however, is that now our child possesses a conceptual structure that will enable her to learn more complete physiological explanations of these functions.

The ways our ideal child interrelates the various body functions she identifies follows a similar developmental progression. Her earliest references to multiple body functions are syncretic in character and manifest a lack of differentiation. One function is associated to another through similarity of parts. A good example of this kind of thinking is the statement that "the heart is something that pumps inside the body. It helps you move around so you will be living. When you breathe it pumps." All levels and forms of body movement are here treated as one relatively undifferentiated function. In contrast, when our child characterizes the body interior in terms of substances and containers, she will treat each body function individually — that is, as self-contained. The heart holds blood, the stomach food, and the lungs air. At this level of thinking there is differentiation without integration.

Following this differentiation, the child begins to integrate functions. The first integrations remain at the level of spatial displacement, where the movements of one body system depend on and interpenetrate with the movements of another system. For example, the child may explain that food goes from the stomach to the blood and, thus, to all parts of the body and that, conversely, one job of circulating blood is to bring food to the body. Later, such interpenetrations are reconceived at the level of transformations or exchanges. With the differentiation of levels of body organization and the concept of continuous transformations, a clear hierarchic integration becomes possible. Nutrition may be conceived at the level of taking in food to the stomach or at the level of cell metabolism, in that order. Nutritive functions at all levels can be seen to depend on circulation and waste removal and on constant neurological and hormonal regulation.

To summarize, conceptions of the body interior begin with a global awareness of body functions and develop by increasing differentiation. There is first a differentiation of structure from function and of various functions from one another in terms of perceptual characteristics, then further differentiation of levels of body organization, specific organic substructures, and transformations. Overlapping this differentiation is an increasingly refined integration of structures and functions. Here there is a movement from fusion based on perceptual similarity to recognition of the joint actions of various organs in the movement of body substances, to hierarchic integration of body functions both at the level of cells and at the level of systems.

This development, in general, is not a matter of replacing childish misconceptions with adult accuracy. Indeed, relatively few of the ideas expressed by children in recent studies have been patently erroneous. They have, however, often been quite limited. Development proceeds by a gradual specification and elaboration of these limited ideas, in which each level of understanding is built on what precedes it.

Using the Theory

The levels of conceptualization discussed in the preceding section are a series of ideal types, and the carefully annotated story about the body interior, used to illustrate, is told by an ideal child. The responses quoted were in fact not those of a single child but rather a composite of responses from many children. The developmental sequence was achieved not by an examination of changes in one child's thought over time but rather by a formal analysis and theoretical ordering of isolated responses taken from the interviews of many children.

Our original questions, however, were not about ideal types. They were about real children and the things they say about the human body. So let us now return to these real children. What do we find when we look at stories they tell about the body interior?

First, we find that two children of the same age often tell very different stories. Consider, for example, two of the five nine-year-olds interviewed for this study. One of them described internal functions in a very global, syncretic way. "The heart," he said, "is what you breathe in. It goes like this. [Child breathes in and out.] The lungs are to breathe in too. . . . Food goes in the stomach, and then it comes in your heart, and then it makes you breathe air. . . . Your heart moves your stomach." The well-differentiated explanation offered by the second of our nine-year-olds stands in sharp contrast. This child said: "Your heart works by pumping blood out to the vessels. Blood goes through your body, some to your head. It doesn't stop. It keeps on going, but I don't know where it goes."

Most nine-year-olds offer explanations that resemble the latter one. That is, most nine-year-olds can differentiate various organs and the actions they perform, and many of them are beginning to conceptualize reversible displacements. However, as the first child's thinking makes clear, not all nine-year-olds have developed to this level. Knowing a child's age does not mean we can predict how he or she will think about the body. There is not a one-to-one correspondence of age to stage, although there is a rough correlation.

Furthermore, when we examine children's stories about the body interior, we find a great deal of variability within each child's statements. Many of the children interviewed were able to discuss the stomach in much more sophisticated terms than they used when asked about the brain and muscles. One quite typical child explained how the stomach transforms food, "mashing" it and turning it to blood that "moves and carries food all through the body," while still understanding the brain only as a spatial container. The brain, she said, is "where you think . . . thoughts come from your brain." To add further to the variability, her explanation of muscles remained a very global one. They "make you strong," she said. We would be hard pressed to assign this child's thinking about the body interior to one developmental stage. Is she at the stage of transformations because that is the highest level achieved? Or do we take the model response and say she is most competent at thinking in terms of spatial displacement?

Developmental psychologists have often suggested that, when thinking manifests aspects of more than one stage, the child is *transitional*. Indeed, all of the children interviewed for this study must be transitional, for they all manifested similar variability in their thinking. But, if all children are transitional, the concept ceases to be discriminating and useful. It might be more accurate to say simply that children do not belong in stages.

The difficulty surrounding the assignment of children to stages should not be surprising. Stages are ideal types, theoretical abstractions of the psychologist. They are designed to articulate the sequence of development, to clarify the ways thought must be reorganized as one moves from thinking as a child to thinking as an adult. Thus stages are conceptual tools. There is no reason that a child's thinking, even about such a circumscribed piece of reality as the body interior, should fit in a single stage. That is why I have chosen to talk about levels of conceptualization rather than stages.

While I do not expect children to fit stages, I do expect the theory of levels to be empirically applicable. First, any individual's thoughts about the body interior, if they develop over time, should follow this sequence of levels. Thus, the theory should help articulate any development that occurs. Second, the theoretical sequence should provide a formal standard by which the thinking of different individuals may be compared, and it should help make sense of age-related differences in knowledge and conceptualization of body organs. Finally, the theory should help us appreciate the sense of an individual child's thinking.

Interpretation of Age-Related Differences. While it may be true that there is no one-to-one correspondence of age to stage, there are nevertheless age-related trends in conceptualization that have been well documented by Gellert (1962), Nagy (1953), Porter (1974), and Smith (1977). The main job we initially set for our theory was to interpret these findings.

You will recall that Gellert categorized children's ideas about body functions and arranged the categories in sequence from those expressed most frequently by younger children to those expressed most often by older children. Overall, as we would hope to find, the explanations characteristic of successive age groups follow a developmental sequence. That is, the ideas peculiar to children under eleven years, relating heart function to global emotional processes, health, and superego, represent the most primitive developmental levels in conceptualization of the body interior. The responses more often given by somewhat older children — for example, descriptions of heart sound, heart action, and the relationship of heart rate to running — represent higher levels of thinking. They define the heart by its perceptual characteristics. Responses that Gellert found to be most common among still older children relate the function of the heart to blood, thus differentiating a body substance and using it to mediate the conception of organ and function. One hundred percent of her thirteen- and fourteen-year-olds and 81 percent of her fifteen- and sixteen-year-olds further elaborated the relationship of the heart to blood in terms of an active heart that pumps blood and makes it circulate (Gellert, 1962, p. 333). Thus the highest category in Gellert's system represents thinking at the level of coordinated and reversible movements.

Considered from a formal developmental point of view, this should not be the highest category. While, overall, Gellert picks up important developmental distinctions, her approach sometimes obscures them. Difficulties arise both in her attempt to trace development through the content of thought and in her use of consensus among older children as her criterion of a high level of development. Relying on content, Gellert groups together the following two statements: "The heart beats; it helps you breathe; each beat has something to do with breathing," and "The heart pumps blood through the system; it brings oxygen to the body." Her criterion was that both related heart action to breathing (1962, p. 334). From a structural perspective, the weakness of this grouping is obvious. The same content may be conceptually quite different, depending on the level of formal development. The latter statement represents a much more highly differentiated conception that gets lost in a content category more characteristic of younger children. Thus, grouping responses by content seems to confound important developmental distinctions and tends to obscure the highest levels of development.

My best guess is that some of Gellert's most developed responses fit into the categories relating heart function to energy supply and to purification and/or renewal of body parts or content. Indeed, responses referring to purification and renewal and implying internal transformations were given rarely, mainly by children thirteen years and older. In her ordering, Gellert places this category below the category of less developed responses referring to circulation of blood, because responses of the former type are rare and her criterion for the highest level response is that it be consensual among fifteen- and sixteen-year olds. But consensus in an age group is not an adequate criterion of development. Apparently, at age fifteen or sixteen, the highest conceptual levels are not yet consensual. Most children this age conceptualize the heart in terms of circulation of blood, an accurate, but still limited, conception shared by many children as young as nine years of age. There is at this time no data to indicate whether the highest developmental levels are consensual even among adults. One might guess that they are not. Again, the point is that developmental levels describe formal sequences rather than statistical norms.

Having looked at age differences in conceptions of organ functions, let us return to the question of why children recognize some organs before others. The literature suggests that almost all six-year-old children know about the heart, brain, and bones, but it is a rare six-year-old, even a rare ten-year-old, who knows what intestines are. Why? Young children first recognize the more perceptually available organs—the heart, which can be perceived when it beats, the bones, which can be felt through the skin, and the brain, which can be identified by the inner speech accompanying thought. In contrast, organs such as the lungs, which are commonly recognized by fifth and sixth graders but not by younger children, are those that, if not so perceptually available, can easily be conceptualized as containers or agents in the displacement of body parts and substances. What about the intestines? They might be seen as containers, but they do not become an essential element in the child's picture of the digestive system until the child can conceive of reversible and coordinated movements—that is, until he or she can talk about the absorption of food into the blood and the diverging pathways of assimilation and excretion. Similarly, the nerves and the liver (the pancreas and so forth) are not commonly recognized prior to adolescence, because they become conceptually necessary only at the highest levels of development. It is only at the level of biochemistry and cell metabolism that the liver must be functionally differentiated from the stomach. It is only when body processes are understood to be continuous and hierarchically integrated that the nerves can be conceived as the messengers necessary to the organization and regulation of body functions.

There is of course an occasional young child whose grandmother has "bad nerves" and whose Uncle Henry has a "real nerve" to say the things he does. Some children, too, after eating chicken livers, wonder whether or not people have livers. But while these children may have heard of nerves and livers, in general they do not know much about these organs, which do not fit and are not necessary to their existing conceptual schemas. The child at the dinner table remains satisfied with the unelaborated knowledge that people, too, have livers. The child whose relatives have problems with nerves maintains a global conception that nerves are related to emotions. Later he or she may learn that nerves are what make you feel heat, pain, and the like. But until nerves are more clearly integrated into the child's existing conceptual schemas, they are not likely to appear in the child's spontaneous identification of the things inside the body.

Finally, let us return to our seven-year-old's drawing (Figure 1) and the observation that younger children often include non-organs such as food and blood in their listing of what is inside the body. This phenomenon may be explained in part by Schilder and Wechsler's (1935) suggestion that the only things the child can be sure are inside the body are those that he or she has seen go in (food) or come out (blood). There does seem to be an additional explanation, however. So long as the child conceives the body interior in terms of whole body functions such as eating and breathing, food is as essential as the stomach is; indeed, it is the more readily conceived part of eating. So food is drawn as what is inside the body. It is only as the child begins to differentiate stations and containers from displaceable substances that he or she consistently draws or lists organs rather than substances. Even then, substances such as food, blood, and air are not entirely eliminated from the conception of the body interior; rather, they are reintegrated. They no longer appear in drawings of structures, but they are integral to explanations of function.

Articulating Individual Conceptions. As a challenge, let us now consider the thirteen-year-old whose story about the body includes what Gellert (1962) finds to be a "bewildering mixture of right and wrong conceptions" (p. 343). The child said, "The lungs are in the throat. One is for eating and one is for breathing. If you held your breath, you'd stop circulating . . . [The lungs] regulate breathing; they held diffuse air into the blood stream through capillaries in the air sacs" (p. 343). If our theory does its job, it should help make this mixture of conceptions less bewildering. It should help make sense of all of the child's ideas, from the most common to the most peculiar.

In general this boy's understanding of breathing is at the level of spatial displacement. He knows that the body takes in air and imagines that the air may be either held or circulated. However, this boy has not differentiated body structures and levels of action clearly enough to keep the various displacements straight. Having differentiated the two body functions of breathing and eating, he recognizes that there are two pathways down the throat; but he assimilates this fact to his knowledge that there are two lungs, not knowing the names of the relevant organs. Thus, one lung is for eating. Furthermore, while he has apparently heard a good deal about physiological processes and knows that air is diffused from the lungs into the blood stream, he does not clearly distinguish the physiological level of organization from other levels of body organization. Thus diffusion of air is equated with breathing as a whole, the functions of respiration and circulation are confounded, and both are fused with gross body actions. Therefore, "If you held your breath, you'd stop circulating."

So the child's explanations fluctuate between global and differentiated in an apparently confused manner. But they are not so confused that they can't be understood and remedied. Having diagnosed the problem, a teacher or physician, intending to help this boy develop his understanding, might begin by making clearer structural differentiations between lungs, stomach, blood vessels, and so on. Then the teacher might trace for him the path of the air we breath, from the nose through the trachea to the lungs into the blood stream to the tissues and back. In other words, the teacher might help clarify his understanding at the level at which he is currently conceptualizing the body interior.

Genetic Application. The preceding analysis leads us directly to the practical usefulness of a theory of developmental levels to anyone (parent, physician, teacher, therapist) who might be in a position to teach a bit of physiology to a child. If the teacher could quickly assess the child's current level of thinking and could anticipate the direction in which it would develop next, he or she would be in an excellent position to start an explanation. If, for example, a child thinks of the heart as something that thumps and holds blood, the teacher could help this child to the next step of understanding that the heart pumps blood and that the thumping is only a part of a larger process.

What is critical in such an application of the developmental theory is sequence. The actual time span of this development may be quite long or quite brief. This time, imagine not a child with typical child ideas about the heart but rather a college student entering his or her first physiology class. He or she is probably able to conceive the body at multiple levels, from cells to systems, and to understand physiological transformations. It is also likely, however, that he or she doesn't know much about the liver, except roughly where it is located, that it has something to do with nutrition, and that it can be damaged by drinking too much alcohol. In other words, our student starts with some very global ideas about the liver. Given a bit of instruction, we might expect this individual to arrive quickly at a high level conceptualization, but we might also expect the "microgenesis" of this conceptualization — that is, its development across a brief period of time — to follow the same sequence as all thought about the body interior. Starting, then, with the rough location of the liver within the digestive system, understanding proceeds with a differentiation of the kind of material it contains, its place in the series of displacements of the digestive pathway, and so on. And behold, an understanding of developmental sequence may be useful to a college professor as well as to a fourth grade teacher.

Cognition and Affect

In studies of cognitive development, affect has often been treated as an uncontrolled factor, a situational variable influencing whether or not the individual will think at his or her highest possible level. Affect presumably interferes with high level thinking, prompting temporary regressions. Emotionally disturbed children are expected to show more variability in their cognitive functioning than do their normal age peers. My observation in the present context is that affect may play a somewhat different role. Consider the following examples.

A nine-year-old boy who was referred to therapy for unmanageable, provocative behavior, aggressive outbursts, enuresis, and food hoarding, stated that it was his mouth that made him hungry. He traced the food he ate down the throat, to his heart (see Figure 2). The child later added the stomach to his drawing, right behind the heart, and said food went there too. Initially, however, he explained that from the heart, some of the food goes into the blood and all over the body. Some goes down to the "blubber" and the "glubber," which he located in the abdominal area. This food comes out your "rear." Finally, some turns to liquid, goes down into the "pits," two sections located at the base of the trunk, and comes out through the penis.

This child consistently conceived body functions in terms of coordinated spatial displacements, and he played around the corners of concrete transformations—quite a respectable level of understanding for a nine-year-old. But at the same time, and more strikingly, he segmented his body, desperately trying to separate nutritive functions—food that goes to the heart—from excretory functions. When I first asked him to draw the inside of the body, he refused to draw anything below the beltline. The names he finally gave the lower body sectors, *glubber* and *pits,* underline their problematic character for him. Although he did also include the bladder in his drawing, he stated that it just "sits there." Thus this child organized his body into good and bad, approachable and unapproachable parts, in terms of his current emotional conflicts.

An even more graphic and compelling example of an emotional factor in the conception of the body interior is provided by the following passage from Nabokov's *Pnin:* "My patient was one of those singular, unfortunate peo-

Figure 2. Drawing of Body Interior by Nine-Year-Old Boy in Therapy

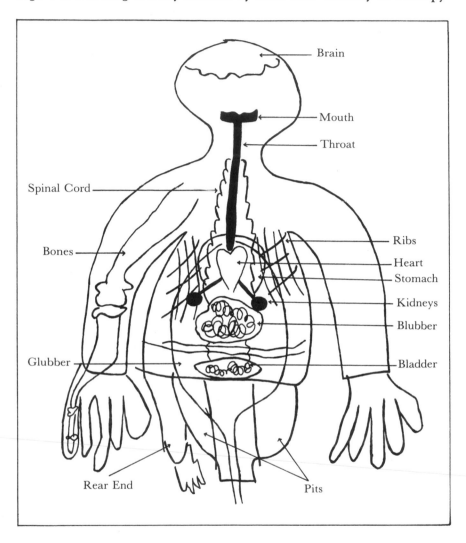

ple who regard their heart . . . with a queasy dread, a nervous repulsion, a sick hate, as if it were some strong, slimy, untouchable monster that one had to be parasitized with, alas . . . . He was afraid of touching his own wrist. He never attempted to sleep on his left side" (p. 20). The conception of the heart here has little at all to do with the structure-function and part-whole relationships that have been the focus of this chapter (although they are vaguely present as an undercurrent). The emphasis is rather on Pnin's regard for his heart, the relationship he sees between it and himself. It is something alien and uncontrollable, something from which he retreats fearfully. Pnin's imagination is controlled by anxiety, and the heart becomes the object of that anxiety.

While drawings of the body interior may tap affective structures in some individuals, I suspect that an even more valuable approach would be to inquire into changes in body functioning. What does it mean when the heart starts beating faster? Does the individual, like Pnin, panic for fear of annihilation? Or does he or she experience it as a burst of strength? How does the individual know when he or she is hungry? How is a hungry stomach experienced differently from a full one? And so on.

There is certainly room for continued investigation into cognition of the body interior. The developmental sequence presented in this chapter needs to be validated, using large samples of children and adults, with more questions designed to elicit conceptions of function — for example, why people have to go to the bathroom. But it is further exploration of the nature and relationships of the cognitive and affective dimensions of imagining the body interior that, to my thinking, offers the more exciting new direction for studies in the conceptualization of the body interior.

References

Gellert, E. "Children's Conceptions of the Content and Functions of the Human Body." *Genetic Psychology Monographs,* 1962, *65,* 293–405.

Nabokov, V. *Pnin.* New York: Doubleday, 1953.

Nagy, M. "Children's Conceptions of Some Bodily Functions." *Journal of Genetic Psychology,* 1953, *83,* 199–216.

Piaget, J. *The Child's Conception of the World.* New York: Harcourt, Brace, 1929.

Piaget, J., and Inhelder, B. *The Growth of Logical Thinking from Childhood to Adolescence.* New York: Basic Books, 1958.

Porter, C. S. "Grade School Children's Perceptions of Internal Body Parts." *Nursing Research,* 1974, *23,* 384–391.

Schilder, P., and Wechsler, D. "What Do Children Know About the Interior of the Body?" *International Journal of Psychoanalysis,* 1935, *16,* 355–360.

Smith, E. C. "Are You Communicating?" *American Journal of Nursing,* 1977, 1966–1968.

Tait, C. D., and Ascher, R. C. "Inside of the Body Test." *Psychosomatic Medicine,* 1955, *17,* 139–148.

Werner, H. "The Concept of Development from a Comparative and Organismic Point of View." In D. B. Harris (Ed.), *The Concept of Development.* Minneapolis: University of Minnesota Press, 1947.

Cathleen Crider is a doctoral student in clinical psychology at Clark University.

Children's ideas about needles, stethoscopes, and X rays can be ordered
in the same manner as their ideas about number seriation,
conservation of weight, or projective space.

Children's Conceptions of Medical Procedures

Margaret S. Steward
David S. Steward

Sammy was not quite four years old when he was knocked off his tricycle by a passing car and sustained a concussion and fractured skull from the accident. When my residents and I interviewed him in the Pediatric Ward, he was a solemn little boy. His head was bandaged, face scraped, and he looked out from two black eyes. I said, "I know you are in the hospital. Why are you here?" He looked around slowly, then answered by pointing to a small, simple Band-Aid on his left arm. "Are the doctors helping you to get well?" "No, the doctors are berry mean . . . the . . . nurse" "What does she do to help you get well?" He explained that she comes in at night when it is "all dark," and touches him on the wrist. He called it his "healing spot." I asked him to show me, and he touched the back of my hand very gently. I asked if he could make me well or if he could make himself well. He said, "Oh, no," and pointed again to the Band-Aid. "My power is all broke," he explained sadly.

This is a child who had experienced, in a very short time, many medical procedures. Most of them, no doubt, were new to him. Using criteria he could not articulate, he had determined that the nurses working the graveyard shift were empowered to cure him and that the procedure of taking his pulse

R. Bibace and M. Walsh (Eds.). *New Directions for Child Development: Childrens' Conceptions of Health, Illness, and Bodily Functions*, no. 14. San Francisco: Jossey-Bass, December 1981

was what was making him well. Of all the injuries he sustained, the one he could see, the cut on the arm, was by far the most serious.

There is little research to help us understand the cognitive components of the child's response. The research literature that specifically addresses the development of children's concepts of medical procedure is sparse, though rich clinical vignettes that include children's spontaneous comments about medical and surgical procedures and hospitalization have been reported for at least forty years (Bergmann and Freud, 1965; Eissler, Kris, and Solnit, 1977; Jackson, 1942; Jessner, Blom, and Waldfogel, 1952; Pearson 1941). Most of this work has focused on the defensive or protective function of children's emotional responses to illness and is based on observations of pediatric or psychiatric staff members. Evaluation of subsequent behavioral adjustments have been based on parental report. There has been relatively little analysis of the level of conceptual development that these responses represent. Furthermore, children's coping strategies and the potential for cognitive and emotional growth, stimulated by the complex experiences that accompany illness in our society, have not been systematically studied. Much of the behavioral disturbance reported by staff and parents may be an attempt on the child's part to solve the cognitive dilemmas and discrepancies introduced by illness, medical procedure, or hospitalization. Shure and Spivack (1978) have noted that what adults often see as disruptive or problematic behavior is really the child's attempted solution to a perceived problem. This chapter is based on a search of the existing literature and on data from our own studies. It is further informed by our experience with children and their families in clinics and hospital settings. In addition, we have drawn on the experiences that our own children have shared with us as they worked their way through broken bones, acute nephritis, pulled Achilles tendons, and poison oak. At the urging of the editors, we have then gone on to speculate. We have created a generic definition of the concept of medical procedures, drafted an instrument that could be used in the analysis of children's responses, and provided clinical examples to flesh it all out. Lastly, we have attempted to reflect briefly on the impact of affect on concept formation.

Initial Research

Duckworth (1979) has maintained that probably the largest single area of research inspired by Piaget's work has been to study the genesis of an idea to see whether its development in the child is really as late as Piaget said it was. Our own work is no exception and came as a result of trying to understand the implications of cognitive developmental theory for the medical care of children. Since it is in real situations that children have most opportunity to test old concepts and develop new ones, our first study (Steward and Regalbuto, 1975) focused on two procedures that young children who receive regular pediatric care commonly experience — use of the stethoscope and the syringe. Two groups of children were selected for individual interview, kindergarten children and third graders. The former we assumed to be preoperational thinkers, the latter to be concrete-operational thinkers. Because we were not interested in teaching children but rather in letting them teach us (so we in turn could teach other adults), we designed a role reversal and encouraged the children to demonstrate the equipment. My coauthor, then a first-year medical student, told the children that he was going to school to become a doctor. He asked them to pretend that he was sick and that they were the doctor and taking care of him. Almost all of the children spontaneously began to examine the instruments; the occasionally shy child was told, "Most kids like to use those things," and by the end of the interview each child had worked with both instruments. Children were encouraged to explain what they were doing and why. Their responses were probed with further questions so that their intents and understanding were clear.

The two instruments evoked some behavior common to all children and some explanations that demonstrated the cognitive differences between the two age groups. Most children used the stethoscope first on themselves, putting the earpiece in their ears and the bell to their own chests; none of the children spontaneously gave themselves a shot, though they obligingly gave one to their "patient." All medical procedures were not perceived to be alike. Their cautious actions with the syringe verified that. All children knew that at least one function of the stethoscope was to listen to the heart beat, but younger and older children differed in what they thought that meant. The younger children described the use of the stethoscope as a tool to determine whether the person is alive or dead. They told us that a doctor listens "so he can tell if it's beating, cause maybe it's stopped . . . . If it's stopped, you'll die." Or the doctor also listens to your heart to see how you are feeling — "to see if I am happy." In contrast, the older children's responses reflected their understanding of a range of heart functions. They were not limited to the essentially binary concepts of alive or dead, happy or sad. They told us that the doctor listens to the heart "to see if it's beating *properly*," "to see if it's thumping *right*," or "to see if you have *too fast* a heart beat."

The younger children associated the use of the syringe with their least favorite part of going to the doctor and were less likely than the third graders to know that the fluid in a "shotter" can prevent illness and/or cure disease. In fact, the kindergarten children did not believe that there was medicine or drugs of any kind in the syringe. Their definitions of medicine were each different ("doesn't sting," "you give it with a spoon," or "you drink it"), but their definitions were also inflexible and did not include the contents of a syringe. Limited to their definitions, they did not believe even when told that a syringe could hold medicine, and even if we insisted that it did, it did not matter anyway, "cause only the needle goes in." How then do shots work? One child said, "It [the needle] goes in your body and it pushes your blood."

We found that the younger children thought quite egocentrically, relating every process and object to themselves; they believed what they saw, and, when they could not see everything, they created an explanation to fill in the gap. The older children could relate this experience to others and generalize. They could understand one object to have several functions and could think about comparative relationships and understand causal sequences. In fact, both groups of children were demonstrating the cognitive structures that Piagetian developmental theory would predict.

Definition of Medical Procedure

It is tempting to try to apply Piaget's (1979) developmental insights to every medical procedure in the book. Given the explosion of techniques in modern medicine, such a series of applications could become the focus for an entire professional career. However, in our case, it became clear, even from the first study, that investigation of children's concepts of medical procedure must include more than just attention to the instrumentation. As a next step, it seemed fruitful to give a formal definition to the concept of medical procedure, including in it the components that appear both necessary and sufficient to understand a child's — or even an adult's — response. Thus, we propose to define a medical procedure as follows: *any procedure conducted or supervised by medical personnel for the purpose of evaluating or modifying health status.*

This definition contains essentially the what, the who, and the why — all of which we believe are essential in order to investigate the view of knowing proposed by Piaget. The first dimension — "any procedure" — may be understood as the body-instrument interaction. It refers to the specific interaction in which the child perceives him- or herself being pressed or interrupted by the world. It includes the range of activities from weighing and measuring to drawing blood to placement on a dialysis machine. The second dimension — "conducted or supervised by medical personnel" — refers to the social role relationships between the patient and the medical personnel, specifically characterized in terms of authority and control. The identification of an interaction as a *medical* procedure requires the involvement of people recognized by the child to occupy a special role. Experienced clinicians know that such recognition can be an important feature of a child's compliance with a procedure. The third dimension — "for the purpose of evaluating or modifying health status" —

refers to the meaning of the procedure for the child, as proposed by the medical personnel. Piaget (1979) would call this third dimension the result of coordinating of relations and would understand it to require rather advanced logical structures. It is this dimension that medical personnel often mistakenly assume to be understood adequately by children, when only its precursors are present.

What follows are scales developed for scoring each of the three dimensions included in the definition of medical procedure. We have drawn heavily from the work of Bernstein and Cowan (1975), Bibace and Walsh (1977), Laurendau and Pinard (1962), and Lemke (1973), all of whom have proposed schedules for rating the structure of responses according to developmental levels. These scales have not been tested with a research population; clinical examples have been drawn from the literature, and whenever possible are verbatim.

Dimension One: "Any Procedure"

Level 0: Lack of Comprehension.
Level 1: Preoperational Thinking. Magical thinking predominates at this level. For example, procedures are defined by such perceptual cues as smell (the pungency of anesthesia or hospital lysol; Plank, 1961), touch (for example, suppositories made a child feel good even when they contained no medication; Bergmann and Freud, 1965), sound ("you get penis-illin if you touch your penis"; Bergmann and Freud, 1965, p. 82). Procedures are understood animistically (for example, "The needle is too mean to me" [Lewis, 1978, p. 18]; "Chad called the respirator 'my friend' and insisted he would take it home with him" [Miller, 1976, p. 6]). There is a lack of discrimination, or overgeneralization, from specific procedure to personnel and even to setting (Katz, 1979).

Level 2: Transitional Thinking. Static definitions of procedures are based, for example, on context ("At one hospital you get babies, at another you get operations, at others you die; Jackson, 1938, p. 58) or time of day ("The 'blood lady' always comes at ten o'clock"); overdiscrimination is more likely than overgeneralization. (Anesthesia was successfully explained as a special 'tonsil sleep' and differentiated from regular night-time sleep when you are tired, Robertson and Freud, 1956; see in addition, Kendler and Kendler, 1975.) A child is more likely to see slight variations as a whole new experience (when a new nurse cannot take his or her temperature or a new doctor cannot find his or her veins). Without reversible cognitive structures a child limited to a soft diet during the first week of hospitalization may not believe that return to a normal diet is a sign of progress but rather that it will cause a relapse (Beuf, 1979).

Level 3: Concrete-Operational Thinking. All procedures are correctly identified, although their functions are sometimes interpreted quite literally (for example, a bone marrow transplant involves the surgical procedure of removing the bone from a donor and transplanting it in a patient; Kutsanellou-Meyer and Christ, 1978). Since the child can cognitively order variables, the sequence of multiple-step procedures is understood. Following the rules of a procedure is very important to the child who cannot easily understand deviation in sequence, short cuts, or substitutes. Often, because of mastery of quantification, the child mistakenly believes the more the better (for example, "I got three shots a day and the other children only got one . . . . My chart is thicker than a phone directory"; Bergmann and Freud, 1965, p. 124).

Level 4: Transitional Thinking. A child can begin to abstract the essence and function of a procedure even with substitutions in equipment, personnel, or sequence of administration. At this level, a child can begin to cope with an emergency and use what is at hand (a ski or tree limb to splint a leg).

Level 5: Formal-Operational Thinking. A child can conceptually coordinate multiple procedures to serve diagnostic or therapeutic functions, can explain the relative efficacy of different procedures proposed, and can imagine a procedure that does not yet exist and describe how it would function.

Dimension Two: "Conducted or Supervised by Medical Personnel"

Level 0: Lack of Comprehension.

Level 1: Preoperational Thinking. At this level, the identity of medical personnel is based on perceptual cues such as clothing (white coat, nurse's cap) or physical setting (the clinic or hospital—where any adult working may be perceived to be in charge). Power of medical authority is seen as absolute. The source of the power is magical (for example, when a doctor is perceived as powerful because he has red hair like the child's father). A child has a sense of personal ownership (for example, the child refers to "my doctor" [Beuf, 1979] or perceives the doctor as working in "my hospital" [Robertson and Freud, 1956]).

Level 2: Transitional Thinking. At this level, medical personnel are often turned into good guys and bad guys, based on the painfulness of the procedures they administer while the child is awake and alert. ("It feels like she's gonna push it all the way in and leave it in. And leave all my brains out broken and terrible. That nurse I *hate*"; Lewis, 1978, p. 18.)

Level 3: Concrete-Operational Thinking. At this level, the authority of medical personnel is respected—though not uniformly beloved. ("They do all the watching business and we do all the ouch business"; Lewis, 1978, p. 19.) The child understands the hierarchy of command—doctor, nurse, patient.

(The nurse "wouldn't pay any attention to what you had to say. She just went right ahead and did what she pleased while you yelled bloody murder"; Bergmann and Freud, 1965, p. 98.) The child understands that authority can be delegated by medical personnel to other persons and is often delighted to accept supervision on self-administered procedures (Partridge and others, 1972).

Level 4: Transitional Thinking. At this level, authority is becoming relativized and sometimes medical personnel are challenged. There is a growing sense of responsibility for self-care. A child can perceive discrepancy between the feelings of medical authorities and patient rights or feelings. ("Nurse said, 'You're big enough to take it without holding hands,' and they said, 'Carlos doesn't need anybody to hold his hand.' But I'm not Carlos . . . . I just hope the nurses might be able to get to know the patients and understand that we have feelings too"; Lewis, 1978, p. 21; see also Flavell, 1968.)

Level 5: Formal-Operational Thinking. A child at this level understands that the authority of medical personnel is relative to the patient's agreement to comply. There can be emotional and cognitive sensitivity to the role of the medical personnel. ("When I give myself my shot, you're doing it from both ends. You feel it from the doctor's side pushing it in, and you feel it from the patient's side going in. This way I feel the pain that you feel"; Lewis, 1978, pp. 19–20.) The patient knows he or she can choose another doctor or choose not to be under doctor's care at all. The patient can accept responsibility for self-care using the doctor's expertise and supervision (Cousins, 1979).

Dimension Three: "To Evaluate or Modify Health Status"

Level 0: Lack of Comprehension.

Level 1: Preoperational Thinking. At this level, the purpose of a procedure is independent of health status ("to crush me," "to steal my blood," "to take my pitcher," "to hurt me 'cause I'm bad," or "so that I can get a doll house"; see Jessner, Blom, and Waldfogel, 1952, for additional examples). There is no discrimination between evaluative and therapeutic procedures—all procedures should make you well or kill you. A child at this level therefore becomes very confused and frightened when a procedure makes him or her sick before making him or her well (Kutsanellou-Meyer and Christ, 1978). A child understands health status existentially as sick or OK in absolute and binary terms, with symptom criteria unique to the child but primarily visible and on the outer body (Neuhauser and others, 1978).

Level 2: Transitional Thinking. The child understands the purpose for selected procedures. Because egocentric thinking still dominates, he or she may still believe procedures are personal assaults ("She hurt me, so I hurt her";

Robertson and Freud, 1956, p. 415). A child understands some gradation in health status (feeling better, feeling worse).

Level 3: Concrete-Operational Thinking. Cognitive skills allow the child to classify procedures according to evaluative or therapeutic functions, but often the child has a literal understanding of a procedure (as, for example, the child who fights the medical technician who wants a blood sample because the technician might find out her secret — that she has "bad blood"; Bergmann and Freud, 1965). Likewise, a child refused to cooperate with a CAT scan of her brain because she believed it would read her bad thoughts,* and "a thirteen-year-old patient questioned whether he would remain small like the eight-year-old donor, since he now had his blood" (Kutsanellou-Meyer and Christ, 1978, p. 129). A child can understand sequential changes in health status if they are explained beforehand (following chemotherapy comes hair loss and a sweatshirt that boldly announces *Bald Is Beautiful;* following steroids comes weight gain and a new wardrobe). Often, at this stage, children need to test out explanations before they believe them. ("Carol on admission talked freely with the psychiatrist about her fear of death. On awakening from anesthesia she expressed relief that she had not died"; Jessner, Blom, and Waldfogel, 1952, p. 158.)

Level 4: Transitional Thinking. At this level, a child can correctly place new procedures in a diagnostic or therapeutic battery and can coordinate the relationship of a procedure to health status. (One may take a blood and urine sample from a healthy child in order to complete a routine pediatric evaluation, as well as taking both samples from an ill child in order to monitor the progress of a disease.)

Level 5: Formal-Operational Thinking. A child understands the probable impact of various procedures on health status and can evaluate probable impact of procedures physically and psychologically on quality of life.

An Epigenetic Framework

It is instructive to separate the child's conception of medical procedures into three separate dimensions. There is an epigenetic organization within developmental theory that suggests the special importance of a particular dimension of experience at a given time while affirming all dimensions of experience to be present in latent form (Erikson, 1964). Figure 1 presents each component of the definition of medical procedure as a part of every stage of development but identifies the component that we believe is most salient for a

*K. Piner, Director, Child Life Unit, University of California, Davis Medical Center, Sacramento; personal communication, 1980.

Figure 1. Proposed Epigenetic Paradigm for Development of Concept of Medical Procedure

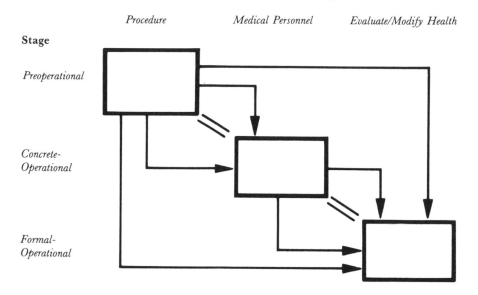

Dimensions of Concept

Procedure   *Medical Personnel*   *Evaluate/Modify Health*

Stage

Preoperational

Concrete-Operational

Formal-Operational

given stage and that, therefore, is the dimension most useful to give focus to that stage.

The events that contribute most to the very young child's conceptualization of medical procedures (preoperational stage) focus on the body-instrument interaction. Authority to implement procedures is assigned only in absolute form, as there is little understanding of the difference between evaluative and therapeutic procedures and no possible judgment about the quality of life. One is sick or well with no comparative judgments made. The concrete-operational child focuses on social relations; in this instance, the role relations amongst the medical personnel and between the child as patient and the medical personnel are critical. The body-instrument interaction will advance to a less animistic, more mechanical and objective level. The right to be involved in the suffering of pain and progress toward health can be mobilized at this stage, as children understand the functions of evaluation and therapeutic intervention. Although death as a final state is understood, quality of life is still too advanced a concept. Rules for administration of procedures and control of procedures are important, rigidly adhered to, and not negotiable. The youth, capable of formal-operational thinking, may focus on the quality of life — that is, the impact of the procedure on his or her sense of self and ability to function in the world. Matters of time, risk, pain are weighed. Medical personnel become consultants. Responsibility for life and death decisions are seen by the youth to rest with him or herself.

Given this epigenetic framework, let us take another look at our conversation with four-year-old Sammy. His selection of the simple Band-Aid reflects the particularity of the preoperational child. Having a Band-Aid put on is the equivalent of being hurt. The sticky pink strip serves as the definition/confirmation that he has been hurt. The fact that he cannot discriminate between evaluative and therapeutic functions is demonstrated by his report that, as the nurse takes his pulse, her touch has healing power and is typical of the magical thinking utilized by children his age (Bibace and Walsh, 1977). Irrespective of the actual power and administrative structure in the hospital, Sammy has determined who is really in charge — in the double sense that he is egocentrically powerful enough to choose who is powerful and that the person who administers the procedure he believes is making him well is the most powerful one. The fact that he believes his own power is "all broken" hints at the devastating emotional impact of illness on young children (Freud, 1952). The epigenetic hypothesis helps sharpen our understanding that the young child essentially leads with his or her body and conceptually takes note of things, experiences, and people as they relate to that body/self. We would rate Sammy's responses as Level 1 across all three dimensions of our scoring system.

Alicia was nine when we last talked to her. In sharp contrast to Sammy's experience, medical procedure for her focused not on the instrument but on her relationship to the medical personnel. Her leukemia had been in remission for the second time, and she had been home from the hospital for three weeks. We talked about "the needles," the all too redundant experience of having blood samples drawn to determine the white count. "It's my body," she nearly shouted, "and I wanted to watch!" She explained that, every time a new medical technician or medical student came into her hospital room, he or she would announce matter-of-factly that she was to lie down flat and turn her head to watch out the window while they went about their work. In other words, she was not to look. However, that was not how Alicia operated. She explained that "there are lots of things you can decide, that don't interrupt the doctor. . . . Like you can sit up or lie down, or you can watch or not, or you can turn to look at TV or your Mom. . . . I *always* watch, after all, it's my body."

Alicia could explain accurately the procedure used in drawing blood. She knew the technical names for the equipment and had none of the fears about "running out of blood" that many young children often express. She understood the numerical range within which her count would mean good news. All of this information had been mastered and was an effective component in her concept of the procedure. She was clear about the authority of the medical personnel and also clear that she had some control as well. She could decide to behave in certain ways that challenged the instructions but, at the same time, would not interrupt or alter the critical elements of the procedure. Elkind (1978) speaks of the concrete-operational child as the rule maker and follower. In fact, for this child, the rules of the game controlled the behavior of the technician and her own behavior as well. She might challenge certain instructions, but she would become upset if there were deviations in any of the more critical steps in the procedure.

Alicia had clearly discriminated diagnostic from therapeutic procedures — for example, understanding that drawing a blood sample would not affect her health status either to make her more ill or to cure her. The critical issues for this child were age/stage appropriate with regard to medical procedures. The procedure was identified, its functions were clear. Her social role relations were central to the cognitive experience of the procedure. It must be said that not every child would take the spunky stand she did, but every concrete-operational child will take some definitive stance relative to the medical personnel with whom he or she must relate. Beuf (1979) has observed hospitalized children develop several response strategies to cope with their relationships to hospital personnel and to sick peers. The wild kid, junior medical student, little hostess, and sick-patient roles are all possible for the concrete-operational child and result from his or her cognitive attempt to establish relationships with personnel with whom he or she must deal. Alicia's concept of medical procedure was centered in her unique vigorous assertion of an active role for herself. There was, however, no challenge to the medical authority. Her responses would be scored as Level 3 across all three dimensions of our system.

An example illustrating the way in which a formal-operational thinker conceptualizes medical procedures comes not from published research or clinical journals but the sports page of our local paper (Bush, 1979). As a result of a brain tumor and subsequent seizure activity, Kim Peyton, a college senior and an Olympic gold medal swimmer, had been put on medication, and it had slowed her time. Knowing she could never be a world-class swimmer as long as she continued to take the drugs, she said, "There is an alternative. Now I'm not saying I'm going to do this, but I could just swim in the AAU meets, and no doctor would have any say over me. The drugs are banned in the Olympics; so if I wanted to try for 1980, I would have to take myself off them anyway" (p. 46). The drawback she also understood: "If I did have seizures again, I would be on phenobarbital the rest of my life. The smartest thing would be to consider my health; after all it is pretty stupid to take a chance" (p. 46). She was quite clear about the interaction of the procedure — in this case the taking of medication — with her body: It would slow her down. In addition, she understood the relationship between herself and the medical personnel; they had given her information and a recommendation, but she was free to weigh that data as well. Her thinking about health status reflected the ability to weight the probable outcomes of different decisions. Unlike the concrete-operational child, she could cognitively manipulate a variety of if-then sequences, without necessarily having to try each combination of possibilities out. Her responses paralleled the psycho-physiological stage of Bibace and Walsh (1977). Her final decision would be based on a weighing of time-limited goals that might seriously impair her health versus the long-range goal of a potentially drug-free and relatively healthy adulthood. Her deliberations would result in Level 5 scores in our system.

It is important to remember that the stages presented here, while invariant, may not be reached by all people. Some people never do take responsibility for the "quality of life" issues regarding the medical procedures proposed for them. Cognitive regression is possible as well, as it is in all socially mediated cognition (Elkind, 1970), though it may be selective (for example, depending on whether a specific illness is acute or chronic or on the amount of time, pain, or financial expense involved). One cannot expect all eight-year-olds to respond the same way, and one cannot be assured that a given child will make the same level of response to every procedure. It is possible, however, to track a child through the stages, given a particular response.

The tracking through the stages is twofold. Within one of the three dimensions, the stage progression is centrism to discrimination to coordination. For example, a young child imputes to an instrument a single function that is an animistic extension of the child's body concept. At the next stage, the instrument is distinguished from the body and can be understood according to its mechanical mode of operation. Finally, the youth may see the instrument function as one of many tests within a diagnostic battery that seeks to identify a still to be diagnosed condition. Similar sequences can be developed for the "role" and "quality of life" dimensions.

Scanning across each stage, the tracking takes place between dimensions from body-instrument to role relations to quality of life. This sequence is epigenetic—that is, each new stage builds on as well as follows the previous stage. Medical roles require the standard application of instruments to give them definition: That is what medical people do. Quality of life decisions require the internalization of concepts and the concern for health and freedom from pain that are central to the medical person's role. Thus, by definition, the core of each of these stage terrains is the prior stage focus.

Impact of a Child's Feelings

Piaget (1962) has said, "Without affect there would be no interest, no need, no motivation; and, consequently, questions or problems would never be posed and there would be no intelligence" (p. 129). It is very clear that the impact of affect on cognition is a topic of sufficient richness and complexity to merit far more than this brief set of comments. We know that a child's feelings may influence the initial construction of concepts and may also influence the rate at which those concepts change. However, conceptual development with respect to medical procedures is a content area more likely than most studied by developmental theorists to be embedded in an emotional context that is heavily weighted with negative feelings (fear, pain, abandonment, punishment, loss of control). For children, these feelings manifest themselves as anticipatory anxiety prior to experience with required procedures; there is often extreme agitation and lack of compliance during a procedure and a slow, difficult readjustment (Katz, 1979).

Even as learning is subordinate to a child's developmental level (Piaget, 1970; Snyder and Feldman, 1977; Turiel, 1969), so negative affect may be differentially disruptive at various developmental levels as well. Jessner, Blom, and Waldfogel (1952) organized interview data from children who had been hospitalized for minor surgery into four age groups. They reported a shifting focus of anxiety with age, noting that the youngest children (three to five years) were more frightened about separation from the family, while the oldest children (ten to fourteen years) were more concerned about enforced dependency and loss of control. Their results suggest that at different ages children select different issues for special concern. Melamud (1976) collected physiological and behavioral measures on children prior to, during, and after hospitalization. She reports that children under seven years of age are more emotional in response to all medical procedures than are older children. This suggests not only a shift in content of concern but also that there may be changes in magnitude of feeling as children develop.

We have noted that children in transition from preoperational to concrete logic are particularly subject to emotional interference when they have been subject to recurrent stress from medical procedures. A review of the literature by Barringer and Gholson (1979) points out that learning, when shaped by negative reinforcement, results in concepts that are quite resistant to change. Thus, concepts that are constructed with partial or fragmented perceptions within the framework of strong negative feelings may stabilize quickly and be difficult to modify with new information or experience.

The child in transition from concrete to formal logic may be vulnerable to emotional interruption also. Schowalter (1977), after reviewing the psychosocial, physical, and emotional impact of illness and hospitalization on adolescents has stated flatly that "regression is the rule and expressions of helplessness are ubiquitous" (p. 504). He observed that sick adolescents act more like latency-aged children. Piaget (1973) has made clear that cognitive and emotional development are essentially two separate systems but that a reciprocal influence also exists. Thus, the emotional regression that Schowalter finds may be correlated with more limited cognitive facility as well. Our own research documents a delay in the ability to handle some concepts with formal logic by adolescents with chronic cardiac disease when contrasted to healthy sex-matched controls (Myers-Vando and others, 1979). In addition, there seems to be a delay in conceptualizing etiology and treatment of illness at the formal level by adolescent siblings of children with diabetes (Carandang and others, 1979).

Most authors agree that adequate preparation for medical and hospital procedures may lessen a child's unwarranted feelings and channel realistic concerns into effective "worry work" (Burstein and Meichenbaum, 1979; Sourkes, 1980). For young children, limited by egocentric, prelogical thought, preparation is exceedingly difficult, and some believe it is impossible (Goslin, 1978) or serves only "to make a child feel something dreadful is about to happen" (Pearson, 1941, p. 720). Well-prepared parents are undoubtedly a critical component, as their emotional understanding is what is most readily transmitted to the child (Solnit, 1977; Visintainer, and Wolfer, 1975).

Melamud and her colleagues (1976) have developed a peer-modeling videotape and have investigated not only how to prepare children but when. They warn that early preparation (five to ten days prior to the experience) for the young child is a mistake and only raises anxiety and misconceptions, while the same amount of early warning facilitates the school-aged child's acknowledgment of the illness. According to Melamud, the slow and deliberate nature of a child's assimilative process is important, for "to truly understand something unknown and fearful, a child needs opportunities to come back to it in his [or her] own time" (p. 14). When a child can teach another, using his or her own past experience, there is potential for both child and teacher to engage in new learning. The book *There Is a Rainbow Behind Every Dark Cloud* (Center for Attitudinal Healing, 1979) reflects the work of Dr. Gerald Jampolsky and the staff at the Center for Attitudinal Healing in Tiburon, California, to encourage children with accidental or life-threatening illnesses to share their own medical experiences with one another and to help prepare, through a phone pal/pen pal program, a child or adolescent for new and potentially fearful medical procedures.

The Carnegie Council on Children has established as one of its goals for change in health care "to increase and strengthen the capacity of communities, parents, and children to act on their own behalf as both health care advocates and health caretakers" (Keniston, 1977, p. 159). This chapter has contributed toward this goal an interactional definition of medical procedures and a caution that the affective component be taken into account in the consideration of medical procedures. As adults better understand children's cognitive capacities, children's participation in health care procedures may become not only less frightening but also may serve as the arena for new learning.

References

Barringer, C., and Gholson, B. "Effects of Type and Combinations of Feedback upon Conceptual Learning by Children: Implications for Research in Academic Learning." *Review of Educational Research,* 1979, *49,* 459–478.

Bergmann, T., and Freud, A. *Children in the Hospital.* New York: International Universities Press, 1965.

Bernstein, A. C., and Cowan, P. A. "Children's Concepts of How People Get Babies." *Child Development,* 1975, *46* (3), 77–91.

Beuf, A. H. *Biting Off the Bracelet: A Study of Children in Hospitals.* Philadelphia: University of Pennsylvania Press, 1979.

Bibace, R., and Walsh, M. E. "The Development of Children's Concepts of Health and Illness." Paper presented at the eighty-fifth American Psychological Association Convention, San Francisco, August 26, 1977.

Burstein, S., and Meichenbaum, D. "The Work of Worrying in Children Undergoing Surgery." *Journal of Abnormal Child Psychology,* 1979, *7,* 121–132.

Bush, G. "Kim Peyton's Swim Through Adversity." *San Francisco Chronicle,* May 15, 1979.

Carandang, M. L. A., Folkins, C. H., Hines, P. A., and Steward, M. S. "The Role of Cognitive Level and Sibling Illness in Children's Conceptualizations of Illness." *American Journal of Orthopsychiatry,* 1979, *49* (3), 474–481.

Cousins, N. *Anatomy of an Illness as Perceived by the Patient: Reflections on Healing and Regeneration.* New York: Norton, 1979.

Duckworth, E. "Either We're Too Early and They Can't Learn It or We're Too Late and They Know It Already: The Dilemma of 'Applying Piaget.'" *Harvard Educational Review,* 1979, *49,* 297–312.

Eissler, R. S., Kris, M., and Solnit, A. J. *Physical Illness and Handicap in Childhood.* New Haven: Yale University Press, 1977.

Elkind, D. *Children and Adolescents: Interpretive Essays on Jean Piaget.* New York: Oxford University Press, 1970.

Elkind, D. *Children and Adolescents: Interpretive Essays on Jean Piaget.* New York: Oxford University Press, 1974.

Elkind, D. *The Child's Reality: Three Developmental Themes.* Hillsdale, N.J.: Erlbaum, 1978.

Erikson, E. H. *Childhood and Society.* (2nd ed.) New York: Norton, 1964.

Flavell, J. H. *The Development of Role-Taking and Communication Skills in Children.* New York: Wiley, 1968.

Freud, A. "The Role of Bodily Illness in the Mental Life of Children." *Psychoanalytic Study of the Child,* 1952, *7,* 69–80.

Goslin, E. R. "Hospitalization as a Life Crisis for the Preschool Child: A Critical Review." *Journal of Community Health,* 1978, *3* (4), 321–346.

Jackson, E. B. "Treatment of the Young Child in the Hospital." *American Journal of Orthopsychiatry,* 1942, *12,* 56–68.

Jampolsky, G. *There Is a Rainbow Behind Every Dark Cloud.* Center for Attitudinal Healing. Millbrae, Calif.: Celestial Arts, 1979.

Jessner, L., Blom, G. E., and Waldfogel, S. "Emotional Implications of Tonsillectomy and Adenoidectomy on Children." *Psychoanalytic Study of the Child,* 1952, *7,* 126–169.

Katz, E. R. "Distress Behavior in Children with Leukemia Undergoing Medical Procedures." Paper presented at the eighty-seventh American Psychological Association Convention, New York, September 1979.

Kendler, H. H., and Kendler, T. S. "From Discrimination Learning to Cognitive Development: A Neo-behavioristic Odyssey." In W. K. Estes (Ed.), *Handbook of Learning and Cognitive Processes.* Hillsdale, N.J.: Erlbaum, 1975.

Keniston, K. *All Our Children: The American Family Under Pressure.* New York: Harcourt Brace Jovanovich, 1977.

Kutsanellou-Meyer, M., and Christ, G. H. "Factors Affecting Coping of Adolescents and Infants on a Reverse Isolation Unit." *Social Work in Health Care,* 1978, *4* (2), 125–137.

Laurendeau, M., and Pinard, A. *Causal Thinking in the Child.* New York: International Universities Press, 1962.

Lemke, S. "Children's Identity Concepts." Unpublished doctoral dissertation, University of California, Berkeley, 1973.

Lewis, N. "The Needle Is Like an Animal." *Children Today,* 1978, *7,* 18–21.

Melamud, B. G. "Psychological Preparations for Hospitalization." In S. Rachman (Ed.), *Contributions to Medical Psychology.* Oxford, England: Pergamon Press, 1976.

Miller, J. A. "Psychological Implications of Total Motor Paralysis in a Five-Year-Old Boy." Paper presented at a meeting of the American Academy of Child Psychiatry, Toronto, October 1976.

Myers-Vando, R., Steward, M. S. Folkins, C. H., and Hines, P. A. "The Effects of Congenital Heart Disease on Cognitive Development, Illness, Causality Concepts, and Vulnerability." *American Journal of Orthopsychiatry,* 1979, *49* (4), 617–625.

Neuhauser, C., Amsterdam, B., Hines, P., and Steward, M. S. "Children's concepts of Healing: Cognitive Development and Locus of Control Factors." *American Journal of Orthopsychiatry,* 1978, *48* (2), 325–341.

Partridge, J. W., Garner, A. M., Thompson, C. W., and Cherry, J. "Attitudes of Adolescents Toward Their Diabetes." *American Journal of Diseases of Children,* 1972, *124,* 226–229.

Pearson, G. H. J. "Effect of Operative Procedures on the Emotional Life of the Child." *American Journal of Diseases of Children,* 1941, *62,* 716–729.

Piaget, J. "The Relation of Affectivity to Intelligence in the Mental Development of the Child." *Bulletin of the Menninger Clinic,* 1962, *26,* 129–137.

Piaget, J. "Piaget's Theory." In P. H. Mussen (Ed.), *Carmichael's Manual of Child Psychology, Vol. 1.* New York: Wiley, 1970.

Piaget, J. *The Child and Reality: Problems of Genetic Psychology.* New York: Grossman, 1973.

Plank, E. A. *Working with Children in Hospitals.* (2nd ed.) Cleveland, Ohio: Case Western Reserve University Press, 1971.

Robertson, J., and Freud, A. "A Mother's Observations on the Tonsillectomy of her Four-Year-Old Daughter." *Psychoanalytic Study of the Child,* 1956, *11,* 410–436.

Schowalter, J. E. "Psychological Reactions to Physical Illness and Hospitalization in Adolescents: A Survey." *Journal of the American Academy of Child Psychiatry,* 1977, *16* (3), 500–516.

Shure, M. B., and Spivak, G. *Problem-Solving Techniques in Childrearing.* San Francisco: Jossey-Bass, 1978.

Snyder, S. S., and Feldman, D. H. "Internal and External Influences on Cognitive-Developmental Change." *Child Development,* 1977, *49* (3), 937–943.

Sourkes, B. "'All the Things I Don't Like About Having Leukemia': Children's Lists." In J. Kellerman (Ed.), *Psychological Aspects of Childhood Cancer.* Springfield, Ill.: Thomas, 1980.

Steward, M. S., and Regalbuto, G. "Do Doctors Know What Children Know?" *American Journal of Orthopsychiatry,* 1975, *45* (1), 146–149.

Turiel, E. "Developmental Processes in the Child's Moral Thinking." In P. Mussen, J. Langer, and M. Covington (Eds.), *Trends and Issues in Developmental Psychology.* New York: Holt, Rinehart and Winston, 1969.

Visintainer, M. A., and Wolfer, J. A. "Psychological Preparation for Surgery. Pediatric Patients: The Effects on Children's and Parents' Stress Responses and Adjustments." *Pediatrics,* 1975, *56* (2), 187–202.

Margaret S. Steward is head of the section of clinical psychology and director of training in clinical psychology in the Department of Psychiatry, School of Medicine, University of California, Davis.

David S. Steward is professor of religious education and director of advanced professional studies at Pacific School of Religion in Berkeley, California. The Stewards are a husband and wife team who have shared interests in research and in the clinical and educational application of developmental systems of learning theories.

Children's understanding of death is mediated by their experience,
feelings, and cognitive capability.

Children's Conceptions of Death

Gerald P. Koocher

Despite an ever increasing willingness by purveyors of the print and broadcast media to portray death in both dramatic and documentary formats, it remains an anxiety-laden topic. This is no less true for adults than for children, since death means loss — the permanent loss of loved ones and, ultimately, the loss of oneself. There are three widely held assumptions about death and how it affects children: first, that children do not understand death, second, that adults, on the other hand, do, and third, that even if children were able to understand death, it would be harmful for them to be concerned about it (Kastenbaum and Costa, 1977). These assumptions, however, are clearly superficial and, in fact, often quite invalid. The understanding of death is an evolving process inextricably linked to our own loss histories. In addition, there is strong evidence that one's level of cognitive development plays a central role in the perception and interpretation of loss events.

Efforts to explore and articulate aspects of death-related behavior in children have followed two distinct pathways. The first has focused on the healthy child's conceptualization of death, while the other approach has dealt with the dying child's awareness of death. The existing body of literature provides general validation for the theory that the child's conception of death follows a developmental sequence regardless of the cultural, emotional, or physical context in which the child is studied, although the content of the child's actual responses is clearly quite situationally dependent.

R. Bibace and M. Walsh (Eds.). *New Directions for Child Development: Childrens' Conceptions of Health, Illness, and Bodily Functions*, no. 14. San Francisco: Jossey-Bass, December 1981

Early Classics

Two important early contributions to the body of literature concerning children and their responses to death are the writings of Anthony (1940) and Nagy (1948). Both studies represented initial attempts to understand the child's conceptions of death from a systematically developmental perspective, and both provide some validation for the theory that these conceptions follow a developmental sequence. Unfortunately, both studies are sufficiently flawed in the methodological sense to make broad generalizability difficult. Interestingly enough, however, the literature on this topic was until recently so sparse that many writers simply accepted and repeated the findings, especially Nagy's, without question or additional investigation (see, for example, Kubler-Ross, 1969, pp. 178–179).

Anthony's study (1940) involved the use of parental records, story completion tasks, and the vocabulary scale of an IQ instrument in which the word *dead* was embedded. Her study population included her own siblings and other children who had been relocated to the English countryside to avoid German air raids in the early years of World War II. Despite these problems, her reports of the children's attempts to integrate their experiences with an understanding of death do supply some interesting insights.

Anthony's main thesis is that the concept of the word *dead* changes developmentally with age, reflecting changes in the child's actual conception of death. She notes a pivotal change at seven or eight years of age and suggests the following hierarchical sequence:

- *First Stage:* The child is ignorant of the meaning of the word *dead*.
- *Second Stage:* The child's interest in the word is linked with a limited or erroneous concept.
- *Third Stage:* The child focuses on associated phenomena in attempting to comprehend the word.
- *Fourth Stage:* The child's understanding of *dead* is correct but limited in scope.
- *Fifth Stage:* The child is able to give a complete biological or logical definition with a general description of *dead*.

The pivotal age is linked to the third stage listed above in the sense that every seven-year-old in her sample gave this type of response, while no five-year-old was able to. Eight-year-olds seemed able to give higher level responses, according to her analysis.

Nagy's (1948) study also presented interpretation problems because of time, place, and sample size issues. Conducted in Budapest at the end of World War II, the study was obviously dealing with a group of children whose background included considerable direct experience with death, loss, and the horrors of war. While these facts tend to limit the generalizability of the response content Nagy reports, her work clearly demonstrates a developmental progression in conceptualizing death.

Nagy's specific findings suggest that children's ideas about death are formed chiefly between the ages of two and nine. She argues for three biodevelopmental stages in that respect:

- *First Stage:* Children under age five regard death as a reversible process (that is, death equals separation).
- *Second Stage:* Between ages five and nine, the child will tend to personify death (for example, regard death as a kind of "boogy man" or "black coachman" figure).
- *Third Stage:* Children aged nine and older regard death as a lawful process (that is, the universality of death is recognized).

It seems highly doubtful that Nagy recognized the role of cognitive development, as opposed to age in and of itself, in formulating her stages. It is also questionable whether she recognized the impact of eastern European folk tales or recent loss histories in the development of the children's conceptions, especially with regard to the content areas she reports.

Another commonly cited paper is an early study by Schilder and Wechsler (1934), although I hesitate to term it a classic because of many methodological problems. Theoretical background for the paper was quite limited and the population of seventy-six children between five and fifteen years old was quite heterogeneous, including six with "organ hyperkinesis," three epileptics, three regarded as "schizoid," nine described as mentally deficient, and the remainder termed behavior problems.

As a point of departure for initiating discussions, Schilder and Wechsler (1934) used a series of eight stimulus pictures including one woman shooting another, a man impaling another with a sword, six human figures that appear to have been hanged, and a strange looking figure reaching toward a skeleton. The conduct of their data analyses are unclear at best and their conclusions that children are quite prepared to kill and often associate death with violence seem obviously questionable. The study is worthy of note more as a very early attempt to address a neglected topic than as an important piece of scientific research.

Death Concepts and Cognitive Development

Much of the scattered research on the child's conception of death published after Nagy (1948) focused on age-related distinctions as opposed to other developmental or cognitive factors. Because most of the early research was undertaken by clinicians, it tended to focus on the content of children's productions about death rather than the form of reasoning underlying the responses.

The reader interested in psychological aspects of death and development of the death concept would do well to begin with three important review works. First among these is the comprehensive chapter addressing psychological perspectives on death written for the *Annual Review of Psychology* by Kastenbaum and Costa (1977). It is important both as a scholarly review citing 169 assorted references and as a documentation of the scientific approach to studying the psychology of death. A second important reference is Duncan's (1979) superbly detailed integration of the research on children's conceptions of death with theoretical material on cognitive and emotional development in childhood. The latter portion of her work also presents death education curricula for use from preschool to high school, including discussion formats, exercises, and readings designed to fit developmentally with the child's needs at each stage of growth. Finally, I would refer the reader to an important new book by Lonetto (1980) that also integrates principles of general child development with research and historical data on children's understanding of death. Lonetto's book has the additional advantage of using illustrative drawings by children of different ages to clarify many of the issues.

Rather than attempt a poor condensation of a literature review, which the writings cited above have already done so well, I will shift to a discussion of my own interests in this area. In particular, I will discuss how my own thinking and research evolved to focus on the child's conception of death as a function of cognitive development.

The initiation of my work in this field grew out of my practice of clinical child psychology. I was assigned to treat a five-year-old who had developed an acute fear of going to bed. In the course of a play session with me, the youngster told a story of overhearing her parents converse about a neighbor who "had a heart attack and fell out of bed dead." She did not know what a heart attack was and was not sure about death, although she knew it was not a good outcome from the way her parents spoke. She assumed that perhaps, if this happened from falling out of bed, it would be best to stay out of bed entirely.

I reasoned that a child's ability to conceptualize death was related to the ability to conceptualize other events and concepts. It seemed likely that the ability to interpret and accommodate data cognitively would be critical to this process. Consequently, I decided to investigate the development of the death concept as a function of cognitive development in the normal American child. My goal was to frame simple, fairly objective questions based on the clinical observations made in the early papers on this topic and to look for differences in the responses of youngsters at different levels of cognitive development.

The developmental hypotheses on which my initial study was predicated (Koocher, 1973) focused on four direct questions. Each child was given a brief screening for verbal intellectual ability in order to assure that lack of such abilities did not confound the data. A series of conservation tasks (that is, mass, number, and volume) and a hypotheses-formation task described by Phillips (1969) were used as a simple means of categorizing children into three developmental groups with respect to Piaget's (1960) general theory: preoperational, concrete-operational, or formal-operational. The four questions asked about death were: What makes things die? How do you make dead things come back to life? When will you die (that is, how old will you be)? What will happen then (that is, what will happen when you die)?

With respect to the first question, I predicted that children at the preoperational level of cognitive development would be limited by their own conceptual processes to providing reasons for the death of people and things that were consistent with egocentrism and adherences to animism (as Piaget [1960] has described). This might include fantasy reasoning, magical thinking, and the sort of special cases that are linked to the child's ideopathic thought processes and personal experiences or beliefs. I expected that children at the concrete- and formal-operational levels of ability would be able to draw on evaluative interpretations of their environment by giving increasingly accurate naturalistic explanations.

When asking about bringing dead things back to life, I expected to find a sharp distinction in the responses of preoperational and concrete-operational children. I expected that preoperational children would indeed present one or more ways by which the dead might be brought back to life. Because the preoperational child has yet to develop the reciprocity of interaction that comes with concrete operations and has no personal experience of death, fantasy must form the only basis for his or her definition. The preoperational child should be unable to tap experiences such as participation in a funeral, because of limitations in what his or her schemata can accommodate. At the concrete- and formal-operational levels, however, children should be able to apply reciprocity skills and learn from the experiences of others, both through conversation and observation. By recognizing that others are different from themselves and have different experiences, these children should be able to imagine the physical permanence of death, despite the fact that they may not have experienced it or had contacts with the death of a friend or family member.

Responses similar to the ones given to the first question were expected when the second one — when will you die? — was asked. Preoperational children were expected to base their estimates on fantasy or highly personalized assumptions, either denying their own potential death outright or producing a grossly unrealistic estimate. Concrete- and formal-operational children, who are better able to accommodate thought processes, were expected to give increasingly more realistic appraisals, ultimately approaching actual life-expectancy statistics, as the ability to appraise the world more independently developed.

The fourth question — what will happen then (when you die)? — was intended as an open-ended probe to explore fantasies by means of a fantasy or projective component. It was specifically intended as a means of support or rejection for the views expressed by Nagy (1948) and others (Gartley and Bernasconi, 1967; Schilder and Wechsler, 1934) which report childhood fantasy material seemingly laced with cultural or methodologically induced stereotypes.

The results of this study are reported elsewhere (Koocher, 1973, 1974b) and were also replicated by the author in a second unpublished study undertaken with a different geographic sample to explore the potential impact of regional differences. There were no regional differences, and the hypotheses outlined above were generally supported.

Using a system of categorizing the children's responses to the question — what makes things die? — judges uninformed of the ages and cognitive development level of the children rated transcripts of their comments on a three-point continuum from *relatively egocentric* to *abstract or generalized* responses (Koocher, 1973). The categories were developed quite simply on the basis of Piaget's observation that the reasoning process evolves from egocentrism to classification and, finally, to abstract principles of constance. In this study, the method of assessing level of cognitive development was the one suggested by Phillips (1969) and also detailed in Koocher (1973). While age in and of itself did not prove to be a reliable indicator of a given child's responses, level of cognitive development did on the first three questions asked, and the judges seemed able to discriminate among the different levels of cognitive ability using only the answers to the question about why things die.

In answer to the question about bringing dead things back to life, only eight of seventy-five children in the initial sample indicated a belief that this was possible and provided instructions (for example, "Keep them warm," or "Take them to the emergency room"). All eight of these children were at the preoperational level according to their responses on conservation tasks (Phillips, 1969), representing 40 percent of the preoperational group in the sample. Since the youngest children in the sample were six years old — that is, near the upper age limit generally associated with preoperational reasoning — one might infer that four- and five-year-olds would be even more inclined to see death as a reversible process. The unpublished replication discussed earlier in the chapter demonstrated that this was the case. No concrete-operational or formal-operational youngster expressed a literal belief in the possibility of bringing dead things back to life, although many were able to talk in sophisticated terms about criteria of death (for example, "brain death," or, "cardiac arrest doesn't necessarily mean you're dead") or about related beliefs (for example, "Do you mean physical death or spiritual death").

When the children were asked to estimate when they would die, mean ages were obtained for the three levels of cognitive development. The mean ages were remarkably close, but the standard deviations differed markedly: preoperational children, mean = 86.6 years, with a standard deviation of 66.01 years; concrete-operational children, mean = 81.3 years, with a standard deviation of 12.68 years; formal-operational children, mean = 81.4 years, with a standard deviation of 9.54 years. Indeed, the estimates did seem to become increasingly realistic as the child's level of cognitive development increased. One classic interchange with a six-year-old preoperational child illustrated this point well. When asked to estimate when he would die, the six-year-old impulsively replied, "When I'm seven." Then he thought for a minute and asked the interviewer for his age. When the interviewer explained that he was twenty-two, the six-year-old proudly asserted that he had revised his own estimate from seven to twenty-three. This youthful attempt at one upsmanship demonstrates the preoperational child's difficulty in fully accommodating environmental data to his own reasoning process.

In answer to the question — "what will happen (when you die)?" — a wide variety of responses were obtained. These were grouped in nonexclusive categories that included references to being buried (52 percent of the children); references to being "judged," going to heaven or hell, or related religious/after-life beliefs (21 percent); funeral plans (19 percent); and predicting the means by which they thought they might die (10 percent). A variety of other responses were also elicited, although, while these are interesting from a clinical or content viewpoint, they generally shed little light on the form of developmental differences. The preoperational children did tend to produce more fantasy responses (such as details of divine intervention), while the formal-operational children tended to emphasize biological facts (such as decomposition of the body after death). The data, however, did not lend themselves to refined categorization and analysis of a rigorous sort.

It is worth noting that not a single child used a personification of death as described by Nagy (1948). No sex or racial differences were manifest in either the original or replication studies, which had a total sample size in excess of 150 children.

The key findings, with implications for future research and clinical practice, include the following (Koocher, 1973, 1974b):

1. Children's levels of cognitive development are not reliably reflected by chronological age in and of itself.

2. Increasing levels of cognitive development are linked with increased levels of abstraction in reasoning about death among children.
3. Advanced levels of cognitive development are related to increased use of reality-based appraisal in conceptualizing death.
4. Magical or egocentric thinking creates a potential hazard with respect to emotional problems in children. Prior to acquisition of concrete-operational thought, misinterpretations related to reversibility of death notions are possible. This may persist as an issue for some children well past age seven.
5. Cultural factors and familial practices at the time of a death vary quite widely, and the pragmatic impact of this variation has seldom been the subject of empirical study.
6. Intellectual processes and information gathering probably represent natural facilitatory coping strategies. Additional documentation of this process in childhood may also be useful.

A recent study (White, Elsom, and Prawat, 1978), conducted without reference to the data summary above, also used a cognitive-developmental model to investigate the development of the child's concept of death among 170 children from kindergarten through fourth grade. Much of the data is consistent with the observation that important changes in the perception of death take place between preoperational and concrete-operational periods. Interestingly, White and his colleagues used a story-telling paradigm with two versions: one in which a kindly old woman dies and the other in which she is seen as unkind. They note that 22 percent of the children in their study seem to view the unkind woman's death as a sort of punishment for her wrongdoing. Since many of the youngsters in this sample were preoperational, this example of magical reasoning is not unusual. In general, the study provides additional support for the contention that level of cognitive development is more useful than grade or age in predicting a child's responses to such questions.

Work with dying children or children with life-threatening illnesses has often led into a discussion of the child's views of death. Most of the authors dealing with the fatally ill child, however, have viewed a child's knowledge of death as something to be acquired by intellectual processes. Spinetta (1974) has addressed in detail the problem of equating the concept of understanding death with the ability to conceptualize its meaning. He points out quite effectively the lack of adequate data, other than clinical anecdotes, for integrating intellectual and affective components in coming to a deeper understanding of how the two interact.

Many authors have reported death-related anxieties in children under six years of age (Spinetta, 1974), a fact that raises the interesting question of how these anxieties might interact with age level of cognitive development among preoperational children. A detailed review of the literature on the psychosocial adjustment of the child with a life-threatening illness traces the evolution of this and related research questions as survival of various childhood illnesses has increased (Slavin, forthcoming). One clear message is that the context and family climate in which death is discussed and experienced is of critical importance in dealing with any death or loss (Bryer, 1979).

While the stage of cognitive development may limit the accommodation of certain data by the child, hence preventing a fully adult comprehension of death (assuming death is ever comprehensible), very young children are able to express death-related fears in the face of serious illness. The preoperational child, for example, will express fear of pain or separation, asking, "Will it hurt to die?" or "Who will take care of me when I die?" In such instances, the child's reasoning is clearly limited by his or her cognitive development. Caretakers must attempt to address the emotional needs, fear of pain and fear of loneliness or abandonment, rather than attempting to address the concept of death from a more advanced perspective.

Theoretical and Methodological Issues

In conceptualizing children's views of death, key theoretical issues have included the matter of whether chronological age or level of cognitive development is the more important factor. Existing data clearly support the view that cognitive functioning is more useful than age in this respect. A key issue in need of further resolution concerns the interaction between affective and cognitive factors discussed earlier. For example, the child who faces death — whether it be his or her own, that of a parent, sibling, or other loved one — will clearly struggle to accommodate this new and painful data. We know little of how this changes the process of conceptualizing death, although we have many clinical anecdotes. For example, two young children ages three and five lost a seven-year-old sibling to cancer. Following a gentle explanation in firm terms by their parents, who assured them that other family members were well, the two were observed playing a newly invented game of "pretend Mommy died." By role playing and mastery, or play repetition, children may cope with some aspects of death that are beyond their cognitive reach in the intellectual sense.

Little has been done to explore the development of the death concept in cases of deviant or atypical development, although the need for such research is unclear except in the case of loss instances such as the two young children who had lost a sibling. In a case of delayed development, for example, it might be predicted that the sequence of concept development is similar but takes place at a slower pace.

A number of methodological issues need careful attention in this area of study, as suggested in the criticism leveled at early research at the outset of this chapter. These methodological factors include: special sensitivity to ethical issues and the child's emotional needs, separate consideration of form and content issues, and extension of existing knowledge through the use of longitudinal studies and new data collection techniques.

Because potential discussions about death necessarily evoke a strong emotional response, a special degree of care and sensitivity is required in the conduct of such research with children. When dealt with in a supportive and straightforward manner, most youngsters are quite willing to share their thoughts about death with an attentive adult or other children. Generally, the adults from whom one must obtain collateral consent are far more anxious about the proposed research than the children themselves (Koocher, 1974a). One must, however, be prepared to deal appropriately with the untoward emotional reactions that may be elicited by questioning and, in addition, arrange to collect data only in a low-demand context. Once, while interviewing a child on the topic of death, I saw his eyes well up with tears. I asked what he was thinking of and he told me how his pet had been run over by a car two weeks earlier. Clearly this was a time for the research to give way to the clinician's focus with supportive comments.

The careful investigator will plan the interview in such a way that stress on the child is minimized and will plan for providing supportive emotional follow-up care if this is needed. My experience with normal children is that such care is seldom needed (Koocher, 1974a), although my clinical experience with cancer patients and their families suggests that it is of critical importance to them and possibly to other abnormally high risk groups. In general, I would discourage individuals without available psychotherapeutic skills and supports from undertaking such investigations.

The social ecology in which the research takes place is a critical factor in influencing the actual content of children's comments about death but should not influence attainment of basic concepts. When interviews take place in a church school, for example, one should not be surprised to find a substantial number of references toward the deity (Gartley and Bernasconi, 1967). When the sessions take place in war zones (Anthony, 1940; Nagy, 1948) or deal with deviant populations and use bizarre stimuli (Schilder and Wechsler, 1934), one cannot claim broad generalizability or practical application with much certainty. Regardless of content responses, however, the child who does not yet understand concepts of constancy should be unable to recognize that death is irreversible.

Most of the existing empirical research on children's conceptions of death has been cross-sectional and gathered through interviews structured with series of questions, story-telling tasks, or requests for drawings. Little or no use has been made of longitudinal data collection or noninterview research methods. The cross-sectional data suggest a progression from egocentrism through centration to a classification stage marked by principles of constancy. This might be expected to precede the mental operations of simultaneous ordering and decentration that make abstract conceptualizations about death possible. One method of exploring this process would be the selection of children at transition points in cognitive development for some longitudinal inquiries about their concepts of death.

Research methods other than adult-child interviews might also be employed as a means for refining our current knowledge in this area. Field studies and similar observational methods using special curriculum materials and peer group discussions to initiate conversations about death could be promising new sources of data. Parent-child interviews and attempts to correlate life experiences with children's accounts of death-related phenomena might also provide methods of obtaining new sorts of data. Still another avenue that has not been explored in detail is that of cross-cultural research on basic themes and conceptual forms regarding death ideation.

Studies of children's conceptions of death have generally relied heavily on face validity for drawing conclusions and, since the focuses vary widely, the scoring and data anlyses schemes often differ. Methods of data analysis in such studies need to be simple and to operate clearly in a way that readily permits replication and adaptation in a variety of settings. When possible, it would be helpful to establish cross-validity techniques and explore a child's answers or expositions on a number of concurrently related dimensions.

The matter of whether the material elicited in the studies described here is similar to spontaneously produced comments and ideas is difficult to address. While it is certainly appropriate for an interviewer to probe and guide responses toward areas of special interest and concern, that process should be the final aspect of the interview. That is, in order to insure maximal validity, the interview and probes should be as objective as possible and all probes ultimately used should be described in detail sufficient to permit replication. Careful separation of data in relation to the questions and probes that elicit them is needed to provide the most useful analyses.

Clinical Issues

Information regarding the development of the child's conception of death has a substantial degree of clinical utility. To begin with, the existing body of data has been integrated to provide a comprehensive death education curriculum from kindergarten through high school (Duncan, 1979). By providing a context and curriculum within which death-related issues can be discussed in a nonthreatening fashion, mastery and coping should be promoted. Public education based on developmental principles can be helpful in encouraging parents to discuss this previously taboo topic with their children in constructive ways (Lonetto, 1980).

In discussing death with preoperational children, for example, it is clearly important to elicit the child's views and draw on his or her experience as much as possible in providing answers or explanations. Supportive comments that address the magical thinking potential of such children also seem indicated (for example, "We miss grandmother too and are very sad that she is dead, but dead people cannot come back to life"). At the same time, even very young children can readily be involved in rituals such as funerals, so long as undue pressure is not applied to force a child's participation against her or his will. Children readily adapt to rituals and can accommodate them well in their cognitive schemata as familiar supportive events, even when full emotional comprehension is not yet possible (Koocher, 1975).

Listening to the questions that are asked from the child's viewpoint is also clearly important. Adult explanations may not be readily interpretable to a child of the preoperational level, and often a key problem is assessing the intent of the questions, rather than attempting a simple factual answer. When a child asks, for example, about why a pet goldfish has died, a response about the fish's "going to heaven" is inclined to be more problematic than a simpler, "We gave him too much food," or, "We let his water get too dirty." However, when the loss is of greater emotional importance to the child, the intent of the question may be better addressed through answers to the unasked questions — "Could that happen to me?" or "Who will take care of me if you die, Daddy?"

When the permanence of death is not yet salient, one must simply repeat the information asked for by the child in a supportive and consistent fashion. The five-year-old sibling of an older youngster who had died of cancer asked her mother what had happened to the other girl on a daily basis for several weeks. At first the mother found that the five-year-old listened attentively as she spoke of how the older child had been very, very sick and how they could not make her better, following with reassurances that the rest of the family was in good health and no danger. As the days went by, however, it became clear that the pattern of continued asking was simply a check on whether the story had changed.

Older children will clearly ask more and different questions. Children of all ages can be encouraged to talk about their feelings or to imagine how other people who experience a loss may feel. By eliciting the views of the children themselves, one has the opportunity to detect and address potential misconceptions.

The care of the child with life-threatening illness has changed radically in the past dozen years from one of benign lies to one of supportive openness (Slavin, forthcoming). Much of this change has been predicated on both clinical and research data about the child's ability to use information about death and about his or her own health status for adaptive coping.

Future Directions

There are several new directions in which the study of children's conceptions of death may continue to make important scientific and social contributions.

Death education curricula will find expanded development and adoption (Duncan, 1979), while children's books and guides for parents that are based on our developmental research will become more available. The subject will become less threatening and better integrated into the child's normal learning environment.

Research on the sources of data used by the child to form conceptions of death will be increasingly important. At the present time the broadcast media and personal experience seem the most important sources of data about death for the child. It will be important to note whether other sources of data become readily usable and salient at different points in development or in different social contexts.

The integration of cognitive and emotional factors in assessing the child's reactions to death and ability to cope with loss is an important area for research. Such work might focus on children who are faced with life-threatening illness and with children who have experienced or are about to experience the loss of someone important in their lives (Furman, 1974). Some interesting propositions along those lines were well illustrated in the volume pulled together to discuss children's reactions to the Kennedy assassination (Wolfenstein and Kliman, 1965). Ultimately, developmental research of this sort will help to provide psychological strategies for facilitating adaptation during death-precipitated emotional crises in childhood.

Studies of interactions among parents, medical personnel, and children when a parent or child is confronting life-threatening illness or death could also be quite useful in improving communication patterns and facilitating coping. The relationship between intellectual functioning, cognitive development, and the ability to communicate on these issues has not been well studied.

The development or refinement of instrumentation, techniques, or strategies for assessing and classifying reactions toward death could go a long way to improve the rigor of such studies. The clinical utility of the data would be significantly enchanced by the development of new assessment and analysis plans that permit a family-based approach to viewing the development of the death concept. Longitudinal research, field or observational studies, and child interaction studies are all potential new avenues of study.

Cross-cultural research, especially in settings where the orientation toward life and death is radically different from Western culture, would be most interesting. Not only would it be possible to explore the development of concepts from a fresh standpoint but it would also be possible to discover what one or another set of cultural beliefs provides in the way of coping abilities during periods of loss and related stress, as suggested by Bryer (1979).

Conclusion

Despite the many taboos that surround direct conversations about death with children, it is evident that even very young children are capable of recognizing differences between the living and the dead. The child's comprehension of death is a complex phenomenon mediated by her or his cognitive capabilities, personal experiences, cultural background, and emotional reactivity. The past decade has seen an increasing interest in research on the development of the death concept in children and erosion of the previous social prohibitions against direct explorations of children's ideas about death.

Research suggests that development of the death concept in children parallels the development of other complex conceptions of the world. The form of such conceptions moves from egocentrism through a centration process toward classification, then to the development of constancy principles and on to simultaneous ordering and decentration, which make abstract conceptualizations about death possible by the time of adolescence. The concept of children's comments about death may vary as a function of experience and social ecology, but the pattern of concept and acquisition (that is, adherences to animism, classification of living and nonliving things, recognition of death's irreversibility, and conceptualization of death as a process of the life cycle) seems relatively consistent.

Attention to specific methodological issues is necessary before quality research in this area can be undertaken, and many new questions remain to be answered. Previous research on the development of the death concept in children has had important clinical utility, and additional research is likely to facilitate both the clinical care of children confronting an emotional loss through death and our understanding of how complex concepts involving multiple components develop in childhood.

References

Anthony, S. *The Child's Discovery of Death.* New York: Harcourt, Brace, 1940.
Bryer, K. "The Way of Death: A Study of Family Support Systems." *American Psychologist*, 1979, *34* (3), 255–261.

Duncan, C. "Teaching Children About Death: A Rationale and Model for Curriculum." Unpublished doctoral dissertation, Boston College, 1979.

Furman, E. *A Child's Parent Dies: Studies in Childhood Bereavement.* New Haven: Yale University Press, 1974.

Gartley, W., and Bernasconi, M. "The Concept of Death in Children." *Journal of Genetic Psychology*, 1967, *110* (1), 71–85.

Kastenbaum, R., and Costa, P. T. "Psychological Perspectives on Death." *Annual Review of Psychology*, 1977, *28*, 225–249.

Koocher, G. P. "Childhood, Death, and Cognitive Development." *Developmental Psychology*, 1973, *9* (3), 369–375.

Koocher, G. P. "Conversations with Children About Death: Ethical Considerations in Research." *Journal of Clinical Child Psychology*, 1974a, *3* (2), 19–21.

Koocher, G. P. "Talking with Children About Death." *American Journal of Orthopsychiatry*, 1974b, *44* (3), 404–411.

Koocher, G. P. "'Why Isn't The Gerbil Moving Any More?' Discussing Death in the Classroom." *Children Today*, 1975, pp. 18–21.

Kubler-Ross, E. *On Death and Dying.* New York: Macmillan, 1969.

Lonetto, R. *Children's Conceptions of Death.* New York: Springer, 1980.

Nagy, M. "The Child's Theories Concerning Death." *Journal of Genetic Psychology*, 1948, *73*, 3–27.

Phillips, J. L., Jr. *The Origins of Intellect: Piaget's Theory.* San Francisco: W. H. Freeman, 1969.

Piaget, J. *The Child's Conception of the World.* Paterson, J. J.: Littlefield, Adams, 1960. (Originally published 1929.)

Schilder, P., and Wechsler, D. "The Attitudes of Children Toward Death." *Journal of Genetic Psychology,* 1934, *45*, 406–451.

Slavin, L. A. "Evolving Psychosocial Issues in the Treatment of Childhood Cancer: A Review." In G. P. Koocher and J. E. O'Malley (Eds.), *The Damocles Syndrome: Psychosocial Consequences of Surviving Childhood Cancer.* New York: McGraw-Hill, forthcoming.

Spinetta, J. J. "The Dying Child's Awareness of Death: A Review." *Psychological Bulletin*, 1974, *81* (4), 256–260.

White, E., Elsom, B., and Prawat, R. "Children's Conceptions of Death." *Child Development*, 1978, *49* (2), 307–310.

Wolfenstein, M., and Kliman, G. (Eds.). *Children and Death of a President: Multidisciplinary Studies.* New York: Doubleday, 1965.

Gerald P. Koocher is acting chief psychologist at Children's Hospital Medical Center, Boston, and assistant professor of psychology at Harvard Medical School.

Index

A

Adolescence, 26–27
Amsterdam, B., 32, 33, 34, 44, 82
Analogies, use of, 24–25
Annual Review of Psychology, 88
Anthony, S., 86, 94
Ascher, R. C., 50, 65

B

Barringer, C., 79, 81
Bergmann, T., 68, 71, 72, 73, 74, 81
Bernasconi, M., 90, 94
Bernstein, A. C., 2, 3, 5, 9–29, 71, 81
Beuf, A. H., 71, 72, 77, 81
Bibace, R., 1–17, 31–48, 49n, 67n, 71, 76, 78, 81
Birth control, 20, 26–27
Birth and sexuality, children's concepts of, 9–29; and adolescence, 26–27; age ranges studied in, 12–19; background studies of, 10–12; and birth control, 20, 26–27; cognitive and emotional development of, 20–22; cognitive stage development in, 19; and communication between adults and children, 22–26; and comprehension of questions, 13–19; and comprehension at various ages, 12–19; and concepts of causality and identity, 12–19; and directions for future research, 27; and education of young children, 23–26; and integration of theory and research, 27; and link between concepts, 19–20; methodological issues in studying, 22–23; methodology used in study of, 12–13; and Origins of Babies scale, 12–19; and physical causality scale, 12–19; and Piaget's cognitive-development theory, 9–10, 11–12, 19, 21, 23; and programs of sex education, 10, 26; and stages of ideas about babies, 19; and theories of sexual development, 21–22; and using analogies, 24–25

Bjorseth, A., 26
Blom, G. E., 68, 73, 74, 79, 81
Body interior, children's conceptions of the, 49–65; and age-related trends, 59–61; and applying developmental theory to various children, 57–58; and articulating individual conceptions, 61–62; cognition and affect in, 63–65; and definition of development, 53; developmental levels in, 52–53; and difficulty of assigning children to stages of development, 58; and distinguishing between internal and external organs, 50; and emotional factors, 63–65; existing literature on, 50; genetic and practical application of theory of development levels, 62–63; and levels of conceptualization, 52–57; and range of concepts, 51–52; and state of child's knowledge, 50–53; and typical example of sequence of conceptualization, 53–56
Breasted, M., 10
Brindis, C., 9n
Brodie, B., 32, 34, 45
Bryer, K., 93, 98
Buckley, L., 33, 34, 42, 44
Burstein, S., 80, 81
Bush, G., 77, 81

C

Cammuso, K., 1n
Campbell, J. D., 32, 33, 34
Carandang, M. L. A., 33, 34, 80, 81
Cherry, J., 82
Childhood and health. *See* Illness, children's conceptions of
Childhood sexuality, 10, 21–22. *See also* Birth and sexuality, children's concepts of
Children's Hospital Medical Center (Boston), 99n
Christ, G. H., 72, 73, 74, 82
Clark University, 7n, 65n

Statement of Ownership , Management, and Circulation
(Required by 39 U.S.C. 3685)

1. Title of Publication: New Directions for Child Development. A. Publication number: 494-090. 2. Date of filing: 9/30/81. 3. Frequency of issue: quarterly. A. Number of issues published annually: four. B. Annual subscription price: $30 institutions; $18 individuals. 4. Location of known office of publication: 433 California Street, San Francisco (San Francisco County), California 94104. 5. Location of the headquarters or general business offices of the publishers: 433 California Street, San Francisco (San Francisco County), California 94104. 6. Names and addresses of publisher, editor, and managing editor: publisher—Jossey-Bass Inc., Publishers, 433 California Street, San Francisco, California 94104; editor—William Damon, Department of Psychology, Clark University, Worcester, Mass. 01610; managing editor—William Henry, 433 California Street, San Francisco, California 94104. 7.Owner: Jossey-Bass Inc., Publishers, 43 California Street, San Francisco, California 94104. 8. Known bondholders, mortgages, and other security holders owning or holding 1 percent or more of total amount of bonds, mortgages, or other securities: same as No. 7. 10. Extent and nature of circulation: (Note: first number indicates average number of copies of each issue during the preceding 12 months; the second number indicates the actual number of copies published nearest to filing date.) A. Total number of copies printed (net press run): 2562, 2540. B. Paid circulation, 1) Sales through dealers and carriers, street vendors, and counter sales: 85, 40. 2) Mail subscriptions: 610, 610. C. Total paid circulation: 695, 650. D. Free distribution by mail, carrier, or other means (samples, complimentary, and other free copies): 125, 125. E. Total distribution (sum of C and D): 820, 775. F. Copies not distributed, 1) Office use, left over, unaccounted, spoiled after printing: 1742, 1765. 2) Returns from news agents: 0, 0. G. Total (sum of E, F1, and 2—should equal net press run shown in A): 2562, 2540. I certify that the statements made by me above are correct and complete.

JOHN R. WARD
Vice-President